GAVEL TO GAVEL

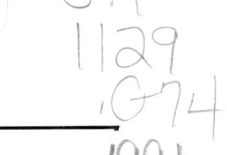

A Guide To The Televised
Proceedings of Congress

★ ★ ★

By Alan Green

A
C-SPAN Publication
Produced in cooperation with
the Benton Foundation

5th Edition

C-SPAN is a non-profit public service created by the U.S. cable television industry to provide viewers access to the live gavel-to-gavel proceedings of the U.S. House of Representatives and the U.S. Senate, and to other forums where public policy is discussed, debated, and decided.

The Benton Foundation, a private grantmaking institution located in Washington, DC, encourages the use of the techniques and technologies of communications to advance the democratic process and works with nonprofit groups to gain an effective voice for social change.

Acknowledgments

A number of people—both in and out of government—were kind enough to offer their time, resources, and expertise, and I would like to offer them my sincerest thanks.
    First, I would like to thank Mike Michaelson, of C-SPAN, whose help throughout the entire project was above and beyond the call of duty.
    Robert B. Dove, Parliamentarian of the Senate, and Charles W. Johnson, Deputy Parliamentarian of the House, were kind enough to review the manuscript for accuracy.
    In addition, I'd like to thank the following people for their assistance at various phases of the project: Sarah Brady, Office of the Senate Sergeant at Arms; George Caldwell, the Library of Congress; John Hackett, Office of the Architect of the Capitol; John Hamilton, Office of the Senate Historian; and Kathy Murphy, C-SPAN.
    The photos on the cover, and pages 11, 13, 16, 19, 24, 30, and 49, are courtesy of the Architect of the Capitol; the photo on page 4 is from National Georgraphic Society Photographer, Courtesy U.S. Capitol Historical Society.
    The drawings on pages 20 and 21 are courtesy Howard E. McCurdy, *An Insider's Guide to the Capitol* (Washington, D.C.: The American University, 1977).
    Much of the contents of this book appeared in an earlier version, first published in 1982 and co-authored by Bill Hogan.

Inside Design: Sharon Rogers, Visual Communications Service, Washington, D.C.
© 1982, 1986, 1991, 1993 by the Benton Foundation

Cover Design: Julie Anne Grace, Grace Advertising, Annandale, Va.

CONTENTS

THE ELECTRONIC EYE — 5
The Merger of Technology and Democracy

THE BIG PICTURE — 6
The How and Why of Cameras in the Chambers

IN CAMERA RANGE — 10
The House and Senate in Focus

BEHIND THE SCENES — 18
A Brief Tour Through the Halls of Congress

THE SCHEDULE ON THE SCREEN — 25
A Guide to Order in Congress

THE LEGISLATIVE LABYRINTH — 37
How A Bill Becomes Law

CONFERENCE COMMITTEES — 46
"The Third House of Congress"

THE AYES HAVE IT — 48
How Members of Congress Vote

A POST-TV GUIDE — 52
Where To Go for More Information

READING GUIDE — 54
Keeping Tabs on Capitol Hill

LEGISLATIVE LEXICON — 55
A Glossary of Key Congressional Terms

THE ELECTRONIC EYE

The Merger of Technology and Democracy

★ ★ ★

It was the great American Revolution—the uprising uniting the 13 original colonies—that gave the United States its unique democratic form of government; now, more than 200 years later, a revolution of another sort is opening up the day-to-day processes and intricacies of this democracy to all American citizens.

It is the communications revolution, a technological insurrection that's stripping away old boundaries and providing Americans everywhere with instantaneous access to one another. Previously, that communication was limited to the town crier, the postal carrier, the telegraph wire, or the reach of the telephone lines crisscrossing the terrain. But now our messages—both audio and video—are sent skyward to satellites hovering above the equator, and subsequently beamed back to towns and cities across the nation.

This technology, which is opening new doors in science, medicine, arts, and entertainment, has also opened wide the doors behind which the United States Congress conducts its business. In the past, the actions of our elected representatives could be scrutinized firsthand only by those making the trek to Washington. (Others had to be content with wading through the carefully edited—even sanitized—pages of the *Congressional Record*.) Even then, the minimal time spent watching proceedings from the visitors' galleries provided little insight into the crucial processes that shape the course of our nation—and the course of our individual lives.

But now, with daily sessions of the Senate and House of Representatives transmitted, in their entirety, by satellite, viewers all over the country can bring the legislative process clearly into view.

With one-third of the Senate and the entire House of Representatives elected every two years, intricate procedures, and complex jargon, Congress can seem as confusing as an unassembled jigsaw puzzle. In fact, it's really not that complicated: the legislative process is governed by a set of rules that can be learned, just as our lawmakers have learned them. Those basic rules—the building blocks upon which Congress constructs our laws—are outlined in this booklet. The rest of the story—the unfolding of countless dramas in the legislative arena—is there before you on the screen. It is the merger of communications and democracy . . . live, and clearly in focus.

Opposite: The view from the topmost balcony within the Capitol Dome, made with a camera hung from a rope across the space

THE BIG PICTURE

The How and Why of Cameras in the Chambers

★ ★ ★

On June 2, 1986, Senate majority leader Robert Dole of Kansas stood on the Senate floor and, with television cameras recording the moment, offered this observation: "I think that today we catch up with the 20th century."

For the proponents of televising Senate proceedings, this day had been a long time coming. More than seven years earlier, the House had opened up its Chamber to the watchful eye of the TV camera—and, in the process, the American public. "In my view, the hallmark of our great political system is an informed electorate," Senator Dole added. "But for the past seven years the Senate has been the invisible half of Congress, off limits to electronic media. Today, that disappearing act ends."

Actually, Dole's historic speech was not totally unprecedented: on December 19, 1974, television cameras were permitted in the Senate Chamber for Vice President Nelson Rockefeller's swearing in ceremony. And television in the House Chamber preceded that Senate first by more than a quarter-century: on January 3, 1947, the House agreed to let the TV cameras roll for part of its opening session, with the pictures seen only in Washington, Philadelphia, and New York. As President Harry Truman looked on from the White House, Representative Charles A. Halleck of Indiana, the House Republican leader, spoke the first words during two hours of televised action. But then it was back to business as usual for the House, with the only spectators those occupying the seats in the galleries overlooking the Chamber.

The issue of allowing television a permanent place in the Congress was first debated in 1944—a time when radio was the dominant medium, color television was still being perfected, and nationwide TV networks were barely in their infancy. Nothing in the rules specifically prohibited the televising of floor action, but the forces opposed to bringing legislative proceedings into the nation's living rooms consistently prevailed.

Congress did permit the nation to eavesdrop on its committee work, however. As early as 1947, television cameras recorded Secretary of State George C. Marshall's testimony before a Senate committee on his plans to reconstruct postwar Europe. Four years later, the nation eagerly tuned in telecasts of the "Kefauver Committee"—the Special Senate Committee investigating organized crime. In addition, TV viewers witnessed the controversial Army-McCarthy hearings in 1954 and, in February 1966, the Senate Foreign Relations Com-

April 1986: Senate technicians install one of eight remotely controlled cameras used to follow floor debate.

mittee's hearings on the war in Vietnam. The House, which experimented briefly with televised committee hearings in the 1950s, enacted formal guidelines for live TV coverage in 1971. Three years later, the House Judiciary Committee's impeachment proceedings against President Richard Nixon were broadcast to the nation.

But while cameras gradually became commonplace at committee hearings, with brief segments shown regularly on television news programs, Congress resisted extending this electronic privilege to floor debate. The arguments against cameras in the Chambers ranged from philosophical to technical considerations: not only would Members be inclined to "ham it up" for the audience, it was argued, but the additional lighting required to ensure sharp images would be an uncomfortable, disruptive factor. The lighting problem ultimately was solved with technological advances in camera equipment, and the House leadership, which had repeatedly resisted the calls for televising debate, succumbed to the wishes of the majority in 1977. The following June, as a precursor to the camera, live radio broadcasts of regular proceedings were initiated. It took a few years of legislative maneuvering and a good deal of testing and study, but the details eventually were worked out and the TV system put in place. Finally, on March 19, 1979, then-Representative Al Gore of Tennessee stepped up to one of the microphones on the House floor and proclaimed the marriage of television and open debate.

The issue of whether to follow the lead of the House continuously nagged the Senate, which is regarded by many as the world's greatest deliberative body.

Opponents of gavel-to-gavel coverage argued that Senators would be forced to "play to the cameras" to impress their constituents. The net result, they claimed, would be longer—and needlessly flamboyant—debate, which would seriously undermine Senate tradition.

But proponents argued that the American public not only wanted to know what the government was doing, but also how it was being done. In 1981, those

★ ★ ★ ★ ★

Until the 63rd Congress (1913-1915), Members of the House had individually assigned seats.

favoring televised proceedings began a concerted effort to rewrite Senate rules; five years later, they prevailed. In March 1986, the Senate began live radio broadcasts, and on June 2 of that year it began a six-week trial run of gavel-to-gavel televised coverage. On July 29, after assessing the experiment, the Senate voted to make television coverage permanent.

The House and Senate broadcasting operations are run exclusively by their own employees, rather than commercial broadcasters. From two separate control rooms in the basement of the Capitol, technicians operating remotely controlled cameras can offer viewers shots from throughout each Chamber.

The gavel-to-gavel proceedings of the House and Senate are beamed sepa-

March 1979: Reporters tour the television control room in the U.S. House of Representatives, where congressional employees control the TV cameras.

Sen. Trent Lott (R-Miss.) leads debate on the Senate floor.

rately to two different satellites, hovering more than 22,300 miles above the equator, by the nonprofit Cable Satellite Public Affairs Network (C-SPAN). Those signals, in turn, are beamed back to cable television systems across the continent for distribution to their viewers. In some areas of the country, where cable TV is not yet available, UHF-TV stations also transmit Congressional coverage.

Often, clips of important floor debates are seen on local or national over-the-air TV news shows. Under rules approved by the House and Senate, the signals of both channels are available to any broadcaster or cable system live or on a taped basis. Members of Congress may purchase copies of tapes, provided the footage won't be used for political or commercial purposes. To help pinpoint a desired piece of footage, time cues, preceded by a box (☐ 1315, for example, means 1:15 p.m.), are printed in the *Congressional Record*.

When the Senate inaugurated its coverage, its channel (C-SPAN 2) was being received by 160 cable systems, with a potential audience of seven million homes. The House channel, having had a seven-year head start, was being received by more than 2,300 cable systems, with a potential audience of some 25 million homes. Those numbers have since increased, and continue to do so. As additional cities are wired for cable, and existing cable systems increase their channel capacity, more Americans will be able to follow the daily activities of both Houses of Congress.

IN CAMERA RANGE

The House and Senate in Focus

★ ★ ★

From the moment the House and Senate convene each day, you'll be watching sometimes deliberative, sometimes frenetic activities. To help you follow the action, here's a rundown of the key players—a sort of "Who's Who" in each Chamber.

The House

The **Speaker of the House**, as elected presiding officer, directs the day-to-day business on the floor of the world's largest parliamentary room: he recognizes Members who wish to speak, rules on questions of parliamentary procedure (which often are critical in determining the fate of a bill), and, from time to time, designates another Member to preside in his place (a Speaker *pro tempore* or Chairman of the Committee of the Whole). He wields the gavel from a seat directly in front of the American flag.

The **Parliamentarian** advises the Speaker and other Members of the House on procedural questions, and rarely is his counsel rejected. His seat on the rostrum is behind the Speaker's chair and to the left, directly below the large bronze scroll. (Note: left-to-right descriptions are based on a head-on view of the rostrum and Chamber, as seen on the television screen.)

The **Sergeant at Arms** or his deputy, seated to the extreme left at a separate table, enforces the House rules of decorum in the Chamber when directed by the Speaker. He is custodian of the mace, the House's symbol of parliamentary power and authority. (During regular sessions, the mace rests on a tall green marble pedestal to the left of the Speaker's desk; when the House sits in the Committee of the Whole, however, the Sergeant at Arms moves the mace to a lower pedestal of white marble.) Beside him sits the Speaker's Page.

The **Clerk of the House** is the body's chief administrative and fiscal officer. He is in charge of recording all votes and certifying passage of bills, processing all legislation introduced after it has been referred by the Parliamentarian, and overseeing record-keeping for all House activities, including daily debates and floor proceedings. On ceremonial occasions, the Clerk occupies the seat to the right of the Speaker, directly underneath the other bronze scroll. At all other times the clerk to the Parliamentarian, who serves as Timekeeper, occupies that chair.

The **Documentarian Pages**, seated to the right of the Clerk, provide Members on the floor with copies of any material to be considered that day. Among

The Senate Chamber, circa 1920

other duties, they also operate the signal system of lights and bells that summons Members to the Chamber for votes or quorum calls.

Members of the Clerk's staff occupy the middle level of the three-tiered dais. On the extreme left is the **Journal Clerk**, who is responsible for maintaining the official record of House proceedings. Next is the **Tally Clerk**, who records all votes and quorum calls, relying most of the time on the House's electronic voting system (which he controls through a computer terminal recessed in his area of the table). He also compiles the daily House Calendar and individual voting records of Members, and receives reports filed by House and conference committees.

If you watch the beginning of a day's session, you'll see the **Chaplain of the House** (or a visiting clergyman) offer a prayer from the Clerk's lectern in the center of the middle tier. Presidents use that same lectern when addressing joint sessions of Congress, but during routine House business, it most frequently is occupied by **Reading Clerks**, who read each item of business brought before the House. **Enrolling Clerks** prepare the word-for-word versions of bills that have been considered and passed by the House (committees prepare the reported bills that come to the floor).

The lowest level of the Speaker's rostrum is occupied by a changing cast of House employees who keep various official records. The seat at the extreme left is occupied by the **Bill Clerk**, who receives not only bills and resolutions being introduced, but also other items—lists of co-sponsors, texts of amendments, and other material to be published in the *Congressional Record*. Members of the House drop these items into the "hopper," a brown wooden box about 15 inches long, 10 inches deep, and eight inches wide.

To the right of the lowest level are the **Official Reporters of Debates**, skilled stenographers whose verbatim notes are used to prepare the account of debates published in the *Congressional Record*. They are considered among the best in the world, working 15-minute shifts while moving about the House floor—often only inches from the Member speaking at the moment.

In the center, **Clerks to the Official Reporters** compile a huge book that becomes part of the text of the *Congressional Record*. They assemble, by number, transcripts, texts of speeches, and all other material representing that day's proceedings.

You may also want to look for the **Timekeeper**, who usually occupies the formal seat of the Clerk (to the right of the Speaker). The Timekeeper watches, computes, and reports on time used during House activities—occasionally making sure "the gentleman from California," for example, who was granted one minute to speak, receives that time and no more. The **Doorkeeper** announces the arrival of special messages from the President and the Senate, and, during special events, escorts official visitors into the Chamber. The Doorkeeper also supervises the cloakrooms adjacent to the House Chamber, makes arrangements for joint sessions and meetings of Congress, and issues all guest passes to the galleries above the Chamber.

Rep. John Lewis (D-Ga.) gives a one-minute speech at the beginning of a House session.

The House Chamber

Directly in front of the Speaker's rostrum are two lecterns, separated by a table. This area, known as the "well," often is the busiest section of the House floor. Each party has its own lectern—Democrats on the left, Republicans on the right—and the Reporters of Debates use the table in the middle. The well is a

★ ★ ★ ★ ★

Only once has the House convened in special session to honor a Senator: November 3, 1977, when special tribute was paid to Hubert H. Humphrey of Minnesota.

convenient place for them to sit or stand while Members are speaking, and other Members frequently mill around to make informal requests of the Speaker or to check or correct their votes as recorded by the electronic voting system.

House Members sit in seats placed in a semicircle around the rostrum—Democrats on the left of the aisle, Republicans on the right. Seats are not assigned, and while many Members have favorite spots, others roam about the House Chamber, sometimes sitting with Members of the opposite party.

In the third row of seats are the leadership and committee tables. The respective party leaders usually sit at one of these tables during debates in which they have an active interest. When bills from committees are being considered, the tables are occupied on opposite sides by the chairman and ranking minority members and staff specialists.

The House galleries are located around and above the Chamber. Most are rarely shown on camera, but occasionally you may be able to see the gallery reserved for the press, above the Speaker's rostrum. Newspaper reporters are seated in the section of the gallery directly above the Speaker's chair; the periodical press is to the left, and radio and television correspondents and technicians to the right. The balance of the gallery seating is reserved for the public, congressional staff, and Members' families.

The Senate

The **Presiding Officer**, addressed by Senators as "Mr. President" or "Madame President," presides over the daily business on the Senate floor from the rostrum, in front of the American flag. The Vice President of the United States presides as President of the Senate, although he customarily assumes this role only on key Administration issues, or if an upcoming vote is expected to be close, since he can only vote to break a tie. In his absence, the President *pro tempore*—usually the Senator of the majority party with the longest tenure—fills that role. However, the President *pro tem* may—and often does—appoint others to act as Presiding Officer. Any Member of the Senate may be designated for this position, although only Senators from the majority party usually preside, normally for one hour at a time.

The **Secretary for the Majority** and the **Secretary for the Minority**, employees of the Senate, have chairs reserved for them behind the presiding officer, on either side of the rostrum. (Note: left-to-right descriptions are, once again, based on a head-on view of the rostrum and Chamber.) These elected officers of the Senate are responsible for providing many support services to their respective leaderships and Members. Their floor-related duties include supervising the cloakrooms, briefing Senators on votes and issues under consideration on the floor, obtaining "pair votes" for Senators, and polling Members at the request of the Leadership. (For an explanation of "pair votes," see page 29.) In addition, they are responsible for assigning desks on the appropriate side of the Chamber, providing a repository for official minutes of majority and minority conferences and committees, and recommending to their respective parties candidates for various boards, commissions, and international conferences whose appointments originate in Congress.

These officers of the Senate are flanked—and assisted—by two other appointed officials of the Senate, the **Assistant Secretary for the Majority** and the **Assistant Secretary for the Minority**.

The **Sergeant at Arms**, or his deputy, is seated directly in front of the rostrum, to the left. He is responsible for enforcing all rules in the Senate wing of the Capitol and maintaining decorum on the floor and in the galleries. In addition, he supervises the messengers, pages, and others who work for the Senate.

The **Secretary of the Senate**, seated directly in front of the rostrum, to the right, is the elected official of the Senate responsible for management of many legislative and administrative services. The Secretary is the Senate's disbursing

FOR WHOM THE BELLS TOLL

On days Congress is in session, a system of electric lights and buzzers is used to inform Members of proceedings on the floor. The clocks in the House and Senate office buildings light up with the respective number of buzzer rings, signaling Members of impending votes or other legislative action. In the House, the signals include:

1 ring—teller vote (not a recorded vote).

1 long ring, pause, followed by 3 rings—the start or continuation of a notice quorum call.

1 long ring—termination of a notice quorum call.

2 rings—electronically recorded vote.

2 rings, pause, followed by 2 rings—a manual roll-call vote.

2 rings, pause, followed by 5 rings—first 15-minute vote in a series, where subsequent votes are to be five minutes in length.

3 rings—quorum call.

3 rings, pause, followed by 5 rings—quorum call in the Committee of the Whole, which may be immediately followed by a five-minute recorded vote.

4 rings—adjournment of the House.

5 rings—five-minute electronically recorded vote.

6 rings—recess of the House.

In the Senate, one long ring signifies that a session is convening; one red light on the right-hand side of the clock remains lighted at all times while the Senate is in actual session. The signals throughout a session include:

1 ring—yeas-and-nays.

2 rings—quorum call.

3 rings—call of absentees.

4 rings—adjournment or recess.

5 rings—five minutes remaining on yea-and-nay vote.

6 rings—morning business concluded or temporary recess.

---

officer, and also is custodian of the Senate's official seal. In the absence of the Vice President, and pending the election of a President *pro tempore*, the Secretary performs the duties of the Chair.

Four officials with various legislative responsibilities sit at the lower tier of the rostrum. The **Journal Clerk**, seated to the left, maintains the official record of Senate proceedings. Next is the **Parliamentarian**, who advises the Presiding Officer and others—including Senate committee staffs and the press—on parliamentary aspects of Senate activity. In addition, the Parliamentarian is the Senate's official timekeeper; his records are often referred to during debate to determine the balance of time remaining. Next is the **Legislative Clerk**, who has the responsibility of reporting all bills, messages from the House, conference reports, and amendments to the Senate. Unlike the House, the Senate does not register votes electronically. All record votes are taken by the Legislative Clerk and his assistants; during some votes, the Legislative Clerk is superimposed in a circle on the TV screen and shown calling the roll. At the far right, in front of the Secretary of the Senate, is the **Assistant Secretary of the Senate**, who acts as the Secretary's chief assistant.

Directly in front of the rostrum are two tables for the **Official Reporters of Debates**, who prepare the material relating to Senate business that will be print-

Senators sit at assigned desks on four tiers around the rostrum

ed in the *Congressional Record*. All proceedings in the Senate Chamber are reported verbatim by a staff of seven Official Reporters of Debates; they work under the supervision of the **Editor in Chief,** the editor of all material in the Senate proceedings. The Official Reporters also process for inclusion in the *Congressional Record* a description of morning business conducted by the Senate (messages from the President or the House, notices of hearings, and the like), and additional statements of Senators, including written statements.

Although these two tables in front of the rostrum are designated for the Official Reporters, they often are occupied by other Senate employees, who keep track of legislation and other Senate business. Included among those at the table might be staff members from the Democratic Policy Committee and the Republican Legislative Scheduling Office.

Senators sit at assigned desks in a semicircle on four tiers around the rostrum—Democrats to the left of the aisle, and Republicans to the right. These desks were designed in 1819, and 64 of them are the originals. (Senators make it a custom of carving their name in the drawer of their desk; the desk traditionally occupied by the senior Senator from New Hampshire has such names as Daniel Webster and Henry Cabot Lodge etched in the wood.) Each desk is equipped with a microphone that Senators either hold or clip onto their jacket pocket when they address the Chamber. A technician, seated in the left-front corner of the gallery, controls the volume of the microphones. At the request of a Senator, a page will bring him a portable lectern from which he may speak.

Party leaders occupy the four desks closest to the rostrum. The **Majority Leader** and **Minority Leader**, who enter the Chamber from the center door at the rear of the room, are seated on the aisle in the front row; next to them are the **Whips**, the assistant floor leaders who keep track of all legislation and try to have party members present when key issues are to be voted on. Committee chairmen have no special tables to work from, but rather occupy assigned desks like all other Senators. When a Senator's bill is pending before the Senate, however, he traditionally will move to the desk of his party leader to direct floor action.

Each day in the Senate begins with the Secretary of the Senate and the Presiding Officer escorting the **Chaplain of the Senate**—or a guest chaplain—to the desk for an opening prayer. Viewers of Senate proceedings also will see a

★ ★ ★ ★ ★

Members of the President's Cabinet are not permitted to appear on the floor of either House to answer questions.

constant flow of other people moving on and off the floor. A number of pages, clad in blue suits and white shirts, sit to the right and left of the rostrum waiting for instructions from Senators. Other pages, bearing messages for Members, move in and out of the Chamber.

Members of Senators' personal and committee staffs also may be in the Chamber to provide information on pending legislation, but the number of staff permitted on the floor is limited. If their expertise is required during debate, they may sit in chairs—brought into the Chamber by special request—behind the Senators' assigned desks; at other times, they may wait at the rear of the Chamber, which is lined with couches.

In addition, floor assistance for Democratic Senators is offered by the staff of the Democratic Policy Committee. These staff members provide information regarding the scheduling of legislation, they act as liaison between the legislative committees and the Democratic leadership, they help arrange time agreements on legislation being debated, and they provide advice on general parliamentary situations.

The Republican Legislative Scheduling Office, under the direction of the Secretary for the Republicans, provides similar floor assistance for Republican Senators. The staff also schedules Republican Senators to preside over the Senate.

Like the House, the Senate has galleries located around and above the Chamber. Newspaper reporters are seated in the section of the gallery directly above the Presiding Officer's chair; one row of seats, to the left of the Chamber, is reserved for the periodical press, while radio and television correspondents have a row of reserved seats to the right. (In both the House and Senate, the media have press rooms, complete with typewriters, telephones, and wire service tickers, just off the galleries.) The balance of the gallery is reserved for the Diplomatic Corps, Senate staff, Senators' families and their guests, and the public.

BEHIND THE SCENES

A Brief Tour Through the Halls of Congress

★ ★ ★

From special control rooms within the Capitol, employees of the House and Senate recording studios operate the unattended color television cameras that capture action in the Chambers. By remote control, these technicians determine camera angles; adjust the sound, lights, and color of the broadcast image; and add brief captions. In the House, six cameras, placed at strategic points in the galleries above the floor, generally are directed at major points of activity below: the Speaker's rostrum, the majority and minority leadership tables, the lecterns from which Members speak, and so forth. In the smaller Senate Chamber, where Senators speak from their assigned desks, eight cameras positioned in the gallery rotate to follow debate from all over the floor.

While the cameras "never blink," they do not cover a significant amount of informal legislative activity around the periphery of the Chambers and in the corridors and rooms adjoining them. Even though access to the House and Senate floors is tightly restricted, people continuously move in and out of camera range. In fact, what you see on the TV screen during important debates may at times resemble controlled pandemonium. Here are a few pointers to help you keep track of what's going on, starting with the House of Representatives:

The young people in navy-blue suits rushing in and out of the House Chamber (they perform similar duties in the Senate) are official pages—high school students who deliver documents and messages, run errands for Members, and help out in various House offices. They wait for assignments, out of camera range, at desks in rear corners of the Chamber (Democrats and Republicans each have their own set of pages).

Behind the railings at the rear of the Chamber are the Democratic and Republican cloakrooms. Here, Members may relax, have a snack, use the telephones, and prepare themselves for the time their bill or amendment will be brought up on the floor. One level up from the House floor are special lounges where Members may read, chat with visitors or reporters, or look over and revise their remarks and galley proofs for the *Congressional Record*. Women serving in the House of Representatives have a special lounge (located between Statuary Hall and the Capitol Rotunda) complete with a few desks, kitchen facilities, and portraits of all women who have served in Congress.

The doorways at the left and right of the three-tiered dais lead to the Speaker's Lobby, a large, ornate room where Members may relax and chat with one another, or with staff members and reporters. The Speaker's Lobby has newspa-

The Senate floor from the presiding officer's vantage point

Galleries reserved for reporters, congressional staff, Members' families, and the public ring the Chambers

The House of Representatives

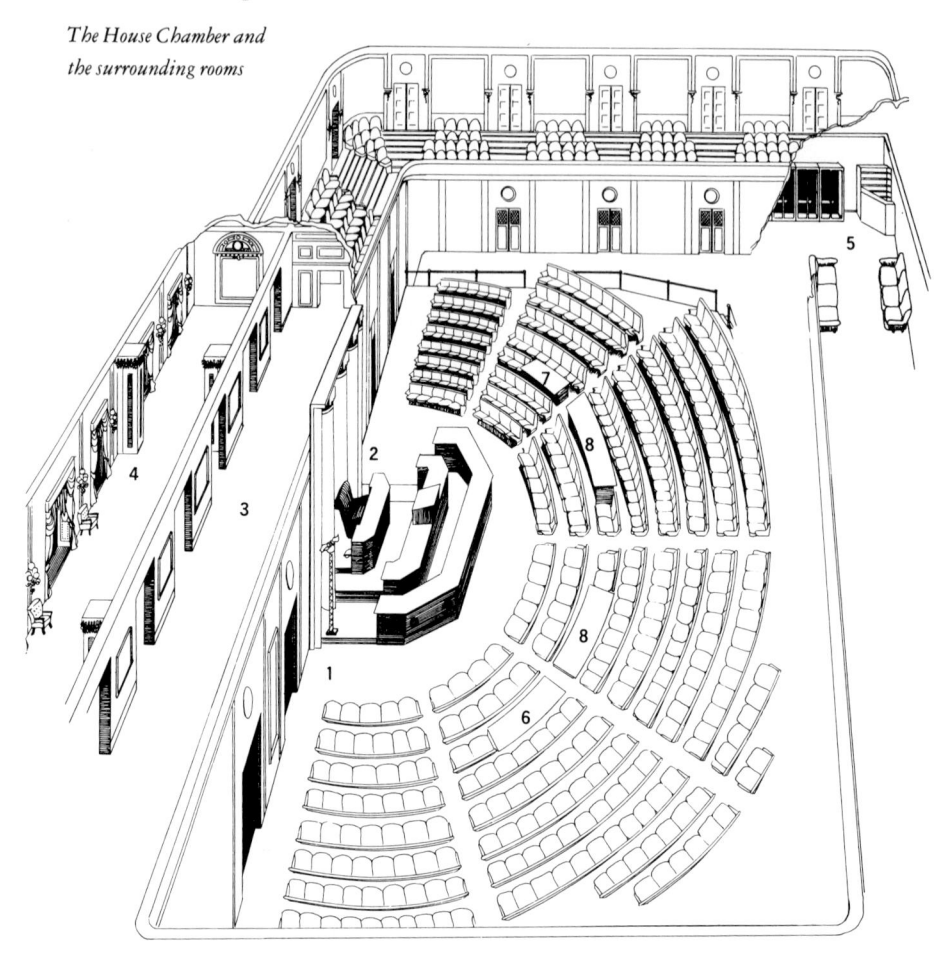

The House Chamber and the surrounding rooms

1. The Mace
2. Speaker of the House
3. Speaker's Lobby
4. Members' Reading Rooms
5. Republican Cloakroom
6. Democratic Leadership Table
7. Republican Leadership Table
8. Committee Tables

pers and a wire-service ticker, but no cameras or recording devices are permitted inside (reporters, in fact, are prohibited from writing about any conversations overheard in this area). Here, Members also have easy access to a special library and reading rooms.

Members of the House and support personnel (stenographers, pages, employees of the Doorkeeper, and so forth) enter the floor from many different locations. Many already will be in the Speaker's Lobby or cloakrooms—just a few steps from the floor. Others will be arriving from the three major House

The Senate

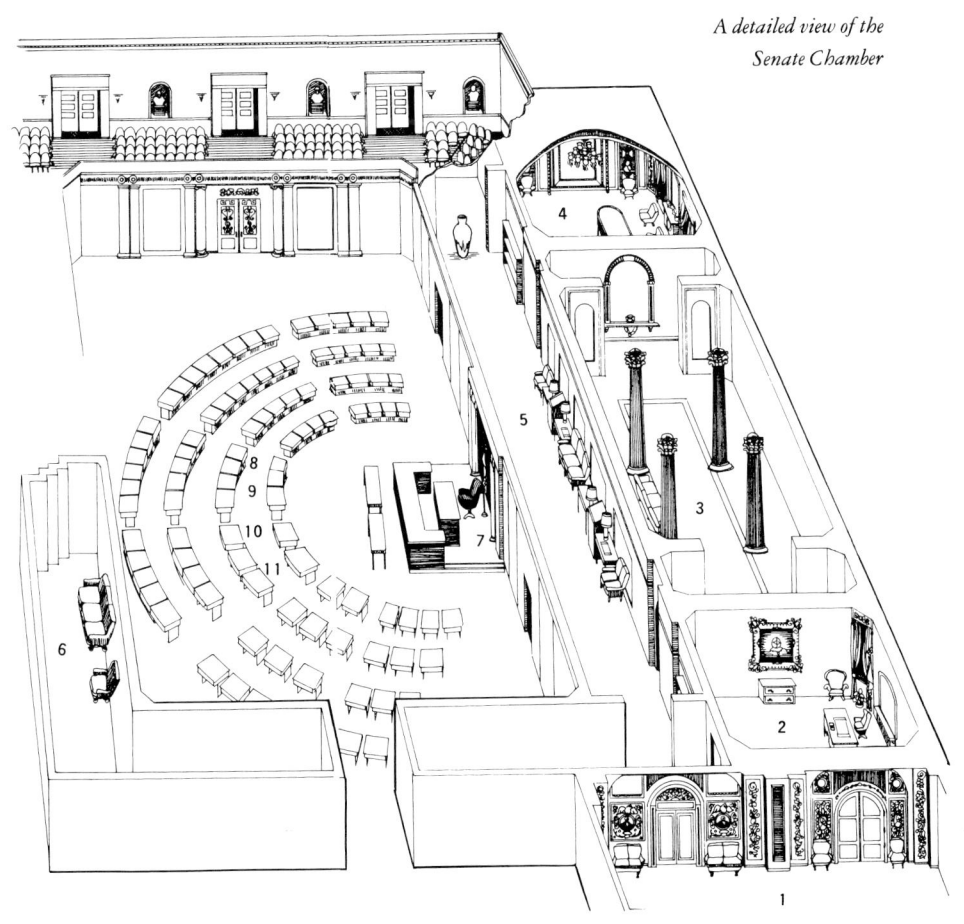

A detailed view of the Senate Chamber

1. Senate Reception Room
2. Vice-President's Room
3. The Marble Room
4. The President's Room
5. Senate Lobby
6. Republican Cloakroom
7. The Presiding Officer
8. Democratic Whip
9. Democratic Leader
10. Republican Leader
11. Republican Whip

office buildings—Rayburn, Longworth, and Cannon—and from other places within the Capitol itself. As a special system of bells (see box, page 15) alerts them to an impending quorum call or vote, many Members will be entering the floor from the far right or far left, corresponding to their party's side. Lobbyists and congressional staffers, cordoned off from the corridors, often wait outside the entrances to have a few words with Members on their way in.

Members cast their votes at any of the 44 voting stations attached to the backs of seats, or in the well by giving a signed card to the Tally Clerk, who enters the vote by using the console on the dais. (See page 48 for an explanation of the electronic voting system.) A special video terminal and printer are located in the rear of the Chamber for Members interested in keeping tabs on various voting statistics.

Like the House Chamber, the Senate Chamber is surrounded by a number of private rooms and offices. Directly behind the rostrum, from which the presiding officer directs floor activity, is the Senate Lobby. Doors on either side of the rostrum lead directly to this room, where Senators can relax, make telephone calls, or check the wire-service ticker. Senators also can speak freely here: the Senate Lobby is considered part of the Senate floor, meaning public access is limited.

Directly behind the Senate Lobby is the Marble Room, another private area officially designated as part of the Senate floor, and off limits to all but Senators. Two ornate ceremonial offices flank the Marble Room: the President's Room to

CONGRESS: THE BASICS

The United States Congress consists of two branches—the Senate and the House of Representatives. The chief function of Congress is the making of laws. In addition, the Senate has the function of advising and consenting to treaties and to certain nominations by the President.

In the matter of impeachments, the House of Representatives presents the charges—a function similar to that of a grand jury—and the Senate sits as a court to try the impeachment. Under the Constitution, top federal officials—including Presidents, vice presidents, Supreme Court justices, and federal judges—can be removed from office by impeachment for such reasons as "treason, bribery or other high crimes and misdemeanors." In order to remove such officials, two-thirds of the Senate must vote for conviction. Throughout history, the House has only voted articles of impeachment against 17 federal officials, 14 of whom were federal judges; some were acquitted, one case was thrown out by the Senate, and three defendants resigned during the proceedings.

Unlike some other parliamentary bodies, both the House and Senate have equal legislative functions and powers—except only the House may initiate revenue bills and traditionally initiates appropriations bills, which provide for funds for carrying on the work of the government.

The Congress meets at least once a year, and has been doing so since 1789, first in New York City and then in Philadelphia. Since November 17, 1800, it has conducted its business in The Capitol, in Washington, D.C.

The Senate is composed of 100 Members. Each state, regardless of area or population, is entitled under the Constitution to two Senators. The Senate is presided over by the Vice President of the United States, who is President of the Senate. In his absence, the President *pro tempore*, who is elected by his fellow Senators, assumes that role. However, the President *pro tempore* may—and often does—appoint other Senators to act as presiding officer.

Senators are elected for terms of six years and are divided into three "classes," so that the terms of approximately one-third expire every two years. The terms of both Senators from a particular state are arranged so they don't terminate at the same time. The one elected first is referred to as the "senior" Senator from that state; the other is referred to as the "junior" Senator.

the left, where Senators often hold press conferences, and the Formal Office of the Vice President to the right.

Doors on either side at the rear of the Chamber lead to the Democratic and Republican cloakrooms, where Senators may relax, make phone calls, or prepare for debate. To the left of the Chamber are the offices of the Secretary of the Senate and others under the Secretary's jurisdiction: the Chief Clerk, the Bill Clerk and Journal Clerk, and the Official Reporters of Debates, whose employees move on and off the floor. To the right of the Chamber are the offices of the Vice President and the Senate Majority Leader, and the Senate Reception Room, where Senators may meet with reporters, constituents, and other visitors.

Although the floor of the Senate sometimes looks somewhat empty, most Senators usually are not far away. Many of them likely will be in one of the three major Senate office buildings—Dirksen, Russell, and Hart—where much of

---

Membership of the House is apportioned on the basis of population of the states, the number fixed at 435. Each state has at least one Representative. The House is presided over by the Speaker, who is chosen by its Members at the beginning of a Congress.

In addition to these 435 Members of the House, there are in that body a Resident Commissioner from Puerto Rico, and one Delegate each from American Samoa, the District of Columbia, Guam, and the Virgin Islands. Unofficially, they also are known as Members of Congress. They have the same rights and privileges as a Representative with respect to attending sessions of the House, engaging in debate, and serving on committees (they may even be committee chairmen). They do not have the right to vote in the House, but may vote in committee.

The life span of a Congress is two years. The Constitution mandates that each body will convene its regular session at noon on January 3, unless by law Congress chooses another day. Each Congress has at least two sessions. In recent years, the first session has usually lasted until just before Christmas, while the second usually has finished up early in the fall, before the new elections. The President may call a special session of Congress, or of either body, if he deems it necessary. A continuation of the second session of Congress that convenes after an election is known as a "lame duck" session.

Both Houses ordinarily meet at noon each day, but either may—and often does—change its hour of meeting. Each House terminates its daily session at its own pleasure, usually by 6:00 p.m.; evening sessions are held when work dictates. Neither House may recess or adjourn for more than three days without the consent of the other.

Bills and resolutions started on their way to enactment, but left unfinished at the end of the first session of Congress, are taken up again at the next session as if no adjournment had taken place. If final action has not been taken at the end of a Congress, however, the measures simply die. Treaties and protocols, which are considered by the Senate only, do not die, but remain from Congress to Congress until disposed of. (Their consideration must be resumed anew at the beginning of the next Congress.) Nominations not acted on in a session die and must be resubmitted to the Senate at the next session. A recess for more than 30 days also requires nominations to be returned to the President.

The mace, the House of Representatives' symbol of parliamentary power and authority, on the marble pedestal

their committee and constituent business takes place. (Senators and Representatives, who often have to beat the clock for floor votes, can get to the Chamber quickly via Congress' own subway system, which links House and Senate office buildings to the Capitol.) In addition, many Senators have private offices in the Capitol, where they can be found conducting business. Others may be in the Senators' Lobby planning legislative strategy; some might be just beyond the Chamber, conferring with lobbyists or staff members, or talking with reporters. There is even a Prayer Room, not far from the Capitol Rotunda, which may be used by Members of the House and Senate.

The televised proceedings of Congress are, in essence, an electronic extension of the galleries above the Chambers. Galleries are set aside for newspaper, periodical, and broadcast reporters; congressional staff; Diplomatic corps; Members' families; and visitors to Congress. Only reporters are permitted to read, write, or talk with others in the galleries.

At some point, of course, you may wish to see congressional proceedings in person. In that case, you'll probably be watching from one of the visitors' galleries, after obtaining a special pass from your Representative or Senator.

THE SCHEDULE ON THE SCREEN

A Guide to Order in Congress

★ ★ ★

Although what happens on the floor of the Senate and the House of Representatives may at times seem haphazard, the sequence of events for daily sessions follows an orderly pattern, in part prescribed by the rules of each body. Both Houses generally convene at noon, because committees and subcommittees meet in the morning, starting as early as 9:00 a.m. (some, like conference committees, often meet while one or both Houses are in session). Here is a brief "road map" to a typical day's activities.

The House

Opening prayer. After the Speaker (or his designee, the Speaker *pro tempore*) brings the House to order, a prayer is delivered by the Chaplain or a visiting clergyman.

The Journal. The Journal, rather than the *Congressional Record*, is the official record of the proceedings of the House. At the beginning of each session, the Speaker simply announces his approval of the Journal of the preceding day, in which case a Member may demand a vote on its approval. A Member also may object to the absence of a quorum, which generally leads to the first roll-call vote of the day on the Journal's approval.

Disposing of business on the Speaker's table. The Speaker may receive special messages from the President or the Senate, he may refer communications from heads of departments and agencies, and he may announce appointments he has made. The Doorkeeper of the House announces and escorts the messenger into the Chamber, the messenger bows to the chair, and announces the title of messages he is delivering. Messages from the Senate might range from special observances—"National Peach Month" or "Afghanistan Day," for example—to votes on conference committee reports and appointments to conference committees. Later, the Speaker will refer these matters to the proper committee or hold them at the Speaker's table.

One-minute speeches. As a courtesy and tradition, the Speaker may recognize Members to address the Chamber on any subject they wish—alternating between Republicans and Democrats—before consideration of regularly scheduled business. Members stand in the front row as they wait for recognition to deliver these "mini-speeches," which last about one minute. During this period, Members also may ask permission to "revise and extend" their remarks and insert various articles, speeches, and the like into the *Congressional Record*.

Unfinished business. On occasion, there may be unfinished business the House was considering when it last adjourned, or which was postponed from a previous day, that will be called up before proceeding with other scheduled matters.

Scheduled business of the day. With most of its traditional housekeeping activities completed, the House then will turn its attention to the scheduled business of the day. In the full House, 218 Members are needed for a quorum; the House may proceed presuming the presence of a quorum, although a quorum must be established when a question is put to a record vote.

At certain times during the day, Members may rise to ask that committees be allowed to meet while the House is in session (an objection by 10 Members denies the request), to file or delay reports, to make one-minute speeches, or to ask other procedural questions. Such procedural questions often take precedence, because they must be decided before returning to the issue at hand.

Deliberations. The Speaker begins deliberation by recognizing a Member who will request legislative action on a scheduled matter, such as consideration of a

Rep. Tillie Fowler (R-Fla.) speaks from "the well" on the House floor.

bill, resolution, or conference report. Opening action may also take the form of a request for unanimous consent to discharge a committee (relieving it of jurisdiction over a matter), or a privileged motion to consider a special rule from the Committee on Rules or a question of privilege, or to resolve the House into the Committee of the Whole (a special process whereby all 435 Members become a "grand committee" for expediting consideration of an important bill).

Parliamentary procedure in the House requires three "readings" of a bill. The first occurs when a bill is introduced and the title printed in the *Congression-*

★ ★ ★ ★ ★

The first woman to preside over the House was Representative Alice M. Robertson, Republican of Oklahoma. When called to the Chair in July 1921, she was presented with the gavel by former Speaker "Uncle Joe" Cannon. The first woman to ever preside over the Senate was Hattie Wyatt Caraway, who, on November 13, 1931, succeeded her husband, Thaddeus, as Democratic Senator from Arkansas.

al Record and the Journal; no reading of the bill, or even the title, actually occurs at this time, however. The second "reading" signifies the beginning of consideration on the floor, and may be a full reading of the text for amendment. The third "reading," usually limited to the title, follows complete action on all amendments.

The rule. Consideration of most major bills or resolutions on the House floor is subject to certain parliamentary requirements, the most important being adoption of a special rule that determines the amount of debate and what amendments and points of order will be in order. Sometimes a resolution establishing a special rule for debate may itself become the subject of heated disagreements—before the measure it permits ever is considered. During this process, points of order, quorum calls, and votes may be ordered before the House adopts a rule resolution governing floor consideration of a bill.

The Committee of the Whole. To speed up consideration of many bills and resolutions, the House frequently resorts to a parliamentary device that allows it to proceed with a quorum of only 100 rather than the customary majority (218). To consider all measures involving taxes or appropriations of money or property, the House must first resolve itself into the "Committee of the Whole House on the State of the Union." If this motion is adopted, the Speaker steps down after appointing a Chairman to preside over the Committee. Essentially, the Chairman assumes the role of the Speaker, recognizing Members, controlling the debate, and ruling on points of order. (When the House sits in the Committee of the Whole, its mace is moved from a pedestal to the left of the Speaker's desk to a white marble pedestal below, a procedure viewers of the televised proceedings may find worth remembering.) At the conclusion of the consideration of a bill for amendment, the Committee of the Whole "rises" and reports the bill back to the House, along with any amendments.

Debate. The presiding officer of the Committee of the Whole allows the principal advocates and opponents of a bill (the floor managers) a certain amount of time ("pursuant to the special rule") for general debate. These floor managers, often the chairman and ranking minority member of the committee or subcom-

★ ★ ★ ★ ★

Henry Clay, at 34, was the youngest person to serve as Speaker of the House. Sam Rayburn, at 79, was the oldest. James K. Polk of Tennessee was the only House Speaker to become President.

mittee reporting the bill, govern who is recognized and how time is allotted. By "yielding" to other Members, they allow supporters of their position to speak or make additional arguments.

During this general debate, and during subsequent debate on amendments, Members make supporting and opposing speeches, ask and answer questions, and challenge the positions of the other side—but always with a formal request for the "yielding" of time or right to the floor, and always with periodic reminders from the Timekeeper through the Chair. Members may either speak from the "well" or from their respective leadership tables.

Amendments. After the conclusion of general debate, the Clerk will read the bill for any amendments. Committee amendments to the pending section usually are considered and debated first. Then, any Member may offer amendments under the "five-minute rule," which allows each Member wishing to speak on either side of the issue five minutes of debate. The debate is governed by the presiding officer, who gives preference to members of the committee reporting the bill.

Members frequently will rise and move to "strike the last word." This is simply a formality that permits a Member to speak on an amendment without offering any substantive changes. If the Member strays from the subject of the amendment, however, another Member may object.

Amendments are offered one at a time, but they may be modified while pending by other amendments or changed entirely by substitute. Even the substitute may be amended. While the entire process often seems confusing, pending amendments are voted on in order and in the same manner as a bill. Immediately after the Committee of the Whole rises after reading a bill for amendment, the Chairman (from the floor beside the rostrum) informs the Speaker of the Committee's action, and the Speaker repeats the information to the full House, which then proceeds to final disposition of the bill.

When consideration in the Committee of the Whole is completed, and after the previous question has been ordered, a Member (normally of the minority party) may offer a motion to recommit—to send the bill or joint resolution back to committee—and the Speaker is required to first recognize a minority Member opposing the legislation. The motion cannot be debated unless it involves instructions to the originating committee. In these cases, 10 minutes of debate (divided equally between supporters and opponents) is allowed before the vote. If adopted, a "straight" motion to recommit has the effect of delaying, or killing, passage of the bill, because from a technical standpoint, it is sent back for further

★ ★ ★ ★ ★

John Nance Garner, Vice President of the United States from 1933-1941, was the only person to address each House the same day as presiding officer. He was presented a watch in the House of Representatives.

deliberations. But a motion to recommit with instructions to report back "forthwith with an amendment" merely permits one final amendment to the bill before passage.

The vote. When it comes time to vote on an amendment or on the bill itself, the Speaker first announces a voice vote and decides which side prevailed. After that, however, a Member from the losing side may ask for a division vote, a recorded vote, or yeas-and-nays (see page 49), or he may object to the vote on the ground that a quorum was not present. If a record vote is ordered, Members will proceed to vote by machine, with the results tabulated electronically and displayed—in progress—on the tote board behind the Speaker's rostrum. The Clerk of the House then announces the vote as well as any absent Members and "pairs." In essence, a "live" pair is a gentleman's agreement between two legislators on opposite sides of an issue in which one agrees to withhold his vote on roll call so that the absence of the other from Congress will not affect the outcome. More frequently, a pair involves two absent members of opposing viewpoints.

After the House passes a bill, a *pro forma* motion to reconsider is automatically made and laid on the table as a way of forestalling this motion at a later date. The reason for this formality: under House rules, a vote is not final and conclusive until there has been an opportunity to reconsider it.

General leave. Following most roll-call votes, the Member who has managed the bill on the floor often will ask unanimous consent of the House that Members have five legislative days in which to revise and extend their remarks on the legislation just agreed to. This allows Members to insert related information in the *Congressional Record* without separately seeking approval.

Deliberation on the next issue. The number of bills or resolutions debated and voted upon changes sharply from day to day, depending on the length of

Electronic tote boards display members' votes.

debates, the length of the session, and the press of other congressional business. One or more entire days may be devoted to highly controversial or complicated issues; on the other hand, a number of bills or resolutions may be disposed of in a matter of minutes through unanimous consent of the House.

Before the House adjourns for the legislative day, a good bit of other routine business—announcements for the *Record*, special orders for the revision and extension of remarks, and notices about certain items of legislation—will be taken care of.

At the end of legislative business on most days, one or more Members may address the House for as much as an hour each on subjects of their choice. These "special order" speeches are arranged in advance by unanimous consent. In this way, Representatives can comment at length on current national and international issues, and discuss bills that have not yet reached the House floor. Often, Members address their special order speeches to a sparsely populated—or even empty—Chamber. But remarks are nonetheless included in the *Congressional Record*, and TV viewers are informed by a message on the screen that the House is considering special orders.

Adjournment. "Mr. Speaker, I move that the House do now adjourn." That's the simple form in which the House ends its official business for the day, and any Member may offer the motion (by custom, it usually is offered by the Majority Leader or his designee). Because the daily adjournment targets are not binding, this motion may come at midafternoon, or sometimes deep into the evening. The House also may, with concurrence of the Senate, adjourn for more than three days to a day certain, or adjourn without fixing a time to meet again ("adjournment sine die"), as it does at the end of each session, for example.

The Senate

To understand the Senate's agenda, one must first understand how Congress defines a new day. A "calendar" day is simply a 24-hour period. A "legislative" day is the period of time following the adjournment of either House until it next adjourns. A recess (rather than an adjournment) in no way affects a legislative day; therefore, a legislative day may continue on for a considerable period of time if the Senate—as it usually does—recesses at the end of business each day, rather than adjourns. If the Senate adjourned each day—as the House usually does—its legislative days would coincide with the calendar days.

This distinction is important, because a number of the rules that determine floor procedure recognize the legislative day. One Senate rule, for example, says that "no Senator shall speak more than twice upon any one question in debate on the same legislative day . . ."

Under two other Senate rules, the first two hours of each new legislative day are called the morning hour. During morning hour, which begins after the Journal is read, the Presiding Officer lays before the Senate messages from the House of Representatives and the President, reports of committees, and various petitions. Then he calls for the introduction of bills and joint resolutions. When morning hour concludes, the Senate resumes consideration of business that was unfinished when it adjourned. But since the Senate usually recesses (rather than adjourns) from day to day, there is often no morning hour, and therefore executive or legislative business can be considered under normal rules of procedure.

With that in mind, here is a typical day's activity in the Senate, following a recess:

Opening prayer. After the Presiding Officer brings the Senate to order, a prayer is delivered by the Senate Chaplain or a visiting clergyman.

Leader time. The Majority and Minority Leaders are recognized by the Chair, usually for about 10 minutes each. During this time, the two party leaders may discuss the legislative schedule, offer their views on policy issues, and conduct non-controversial business by unanimous consent. Or, if they wish, they may yield all or part of their time to other Senators.

Special orders. Following recognition of the two leaders, other Senators may be recognized to speak on any subject of their choosing. These opportunities to speak are called "special orders," and are usually arranged by unanimous consent requests made by the Majority Leader at the end of the previous day's session.

Routine morning business. The Majority Leader usually arranges by unanimous consent for a period of transacting "routine morning business" that fol-

★ ★ ★ ★ ★

In addition to political activities, the old Hall of Representatives in the Capitol, which preceded the present Chamber, was used for Sunday religious services, with the Speaker's desk used as a pulpit.

lows the speeches made under special orders. Senators also make brief statements during this period, the length of which can change from day to day, depending on the legislative schedule. Also by unanimous consent, there may be other periods for transacting morning business during the course of the day when there is time available and when Senators wish to speak on subjects unrelated to the pending bill. In fact, additional time for "routine morning business" can be requested at any hour the Senate is in session.

The Calendar of Business. At the conclusion of morning business, the Senate turns its attention to the scheduled business of the day—whatever bill was pending when the Senate recessed, or other legislative or executive business. The Presiding Officer simply announces that the time for morning business has expired, and the Senate begins its deliberations.

The Constitution requires that a quorum—or majority—of all Senators be present to conduct business on the floor. Even though Senators have many responsibilities that frequently keep them from the floor, the Senate presumes that a quorum is present unless a quorum call demonstrates that it is not.

A Senator who has been recognized may suggest the absence of a quorum at almost any time; a clerk then begins to call the roll of the Senators. (A message informs TV viewers that the Senate is conducting a quorum call.) Senators may not debate or conduct business while a quorum call is in progress. If a majority of Senators do not appear and respond to their names, the Senate can only adjourn or recess, or await the arrival of additional Senators. However, most quorum calls end by unanimous consent before the clerk completes the call of the roll and the absence of a quorum is demonstrated.

The reason is that most quorum calls are not really intended to determine if a quorum is present; rather, the purpose is usually to suspend floor activity temporarily. The absence of a quorum may be suggested, for example, if the Majority Leader wants to meet with several Senators on the floor about a possible

Sen. Dianne Feinstein (D-Calif.) speaks from her desk on the Senate floor.

unanimous consent agreement, or if the floor manager of a bill wants to discuss a compromise alternative to an amendment that has been offered. In short, the time consumed by many quorum calls permits discussions that would be far more difficult to hold under the rules of formal Senate debate.

Debate. Unlike the House, the Senate's rules place greater emphasis on the rights of individual Senators—and, therefore, of those with minority views—than on the powers of the majority. This is perhaps most evident in debate.

When a bill is called up for floor consideration, opening statements usually are made by the two floor managers—the chairman and ranking minority member of the committee (or sometimes the subcommittee) that reported the bill—and often by other Senators as well. These statements lay the groundwork for the debate that follows, describing the purposes and provisions of the bill, the state of current law, the developments that make new legislation desirable or necessary, and the major points of controversy.

Senate rules dictate that Members may only speak twice on a matter each legislative day; at the same time, however, the rules impose no limits whatsoever on the number of Senators who may make those two speeches, nor on the length of the speeches. In fact, there are few Senate rules that limit the right to debate, and no rules that permit a majority of the Senate to end a debate whenever it is ready to vote on a bill, amendment, or other question being considered. When Senators are recognized by the Presiding Officer, they usually may speak for as long as they wish. Furthermore, questions generally cannot be put to a vote as long as there are Senators who still wish to make the speeches permitted by the rules.

Such rules in the Senate create the possibility of filibuster. Individual Senators or groups adamantly opposed to a bill or amendment may speak against it at great length, thus postponing final consideration. Opposing Senators can also delay final floor action by offering numerous amendments and motions, insisting that amendments be read in full, demanding roll-call votes on amendments and motions, and other procedures.

The only formal procedure to break a filibuster is to "invoke cloture," which requires the support of at least three-fifths of the Senate. This vote—if successful—does not cut off consideration, but rather limits it to a maximum of 30 additional hours.

But because debate is such an integral part of Senate history and procedure, a vote to invoke cloture is rare. By the same token, filibusters are the exception, rather than the rule. If Senators filibustered every bill they opposed, the Senate could not meet its constitutional responsibilities in a timely fashion, and it could not respond effectively to pressing national needs. Furthermore, Senators real-

★ ★ ★ ★ ★

On September 5, 1975, Chief Frank Fools Crow, of the Oglala Sioux Indian Tribe, offered the first prayer ever given in the Senate by an American Indian. Dressed in full tribal garb, he spoke in the Sioux language; his words were translated into English by another Sioux Indian.

ize that if they used the filibuster regularly against every bill they opposed, other Senators would be likely to do the same, and every Senator's legislative objectives would be jeopardized. The filibuster, then, is usually a tactic of last resort.

Amendments. Unlike the House, the Senate has no rule requiring that amendments offered on the floor be germane—or relevant—to the bill being considered. (The only exceptions are amendments to general appropriations and budget bills, and matters being considered under cloture.) This means that Senators are free to propose "riders"—amendments proposing substantive legislation—on any subject to any bill being considered. In fact, a Senator can offer an entire bill—on a totally unrelated matter—as a floor amendment to another measure.

As soon as a bill is before the Senate, it is open to amendments. The first amendments considered are those recommended by the committees reporting the bill. As each committee amendment is being debated, Senators may propose amendments to it and to the part of the bill the committee amendment would change; the Senate votes on any such amendments before it votes on the committee amendment itself. After that, Senators may offer amendments in any order to any part of the bill that has not already been amended.

> ## Amendments and Substitutes
>
> The procedure followed in Congress for amending a bill may at first appear complicated, particularly if a viewer tunes in during floor action, but it follows a specific routine. Up to four alternative amendments to a bill or resolution may be pending simultaneously, as follows: 1) the original amendment; 2) an amendment to the original amendment; 3) a substitute for the original amendment; and 4) an amendment to the substitute.
>
> The order of voting is as follows: the first vote occurs on the amendment to the original amendment; next, the amendment to the substitute is voted on; the substitute as amended or not follows; and finally, a vote occurs on the original amendment as modified by its own amendment or substitute.

After a Senator offers an amendment, it must be read, unless the Senate dispenses with the reading by unanimous consent. The Senate then debates the amendment and may dispose of it either by voting "up or down" on the amendment itself, or by voting to table it. Amendments may also be amended, and, like the House, the Senate follows a definite order when considering amendments (see Box, above).

The conditions for debating an amendment depend on whether or not there is a time limitation placed on its consideration. Such "time agreements" are frequently worked out by committee chairmen and party leaders, to ensure that the Senate does not debate endlessly each measure it considers. (For a fuller explanation of time agreements, see page 44.) If there is no such limitation, each Senator may debate the amendment for as long as he or she pleases, subject only to the rule limiting each Senator to two speeches on a question each legislative day.

When all committee amendments and floor amendments offered by Senators have been disposed of, the bill is ordered engrossed—that is, printed with all such changes—and read a third time, thereby ending the amendatory process.

The vote. Most bills are passed by a voice vote only. When a doubt is raised, however, any Senator may—before the result is announced— request a division vote. (For a detailed explanation of Senate voting procedures, see page 50.) Before the result of a voice or division vote has been announced, a roll-call vote may be demanded by one-fifth of the Senators present. (No fewer than 11 Senators must demand such a vote.) A simple majority is necessary for passage.

In the case of a yea-and-nay vote, any Senator who voted with the prevailing side, or who did not vote, may make a motion within the next two days to reconsider the action—a parliamentary tactic to ensure that the decision will stand. (Such motions are usually made immediately following the vote.) If the measure was passed without a recorded vote, any Senator may make the motion to reconsider. Another Senator then moves to table the motion to reconsider, and if the Senate, by a voice vote, approves the motion to table, that constitutes a final

A congressional employee captions Senate debate for hearing impaired viewers. Both House and Senate floor debates are now closed captioned.

action. But if the Senate votes to grant the motion to reconsider, it may, by a majority vote, either affirm its action, which then becomes final, or reverse it.

Deliberation on the next issue. Following a vote, the Senate may consider other legislation, it may transact routine morning business, it may consider executive matters, or it may recess or adjourn.

Before the Senate does recess each day, a good bit of other routine business will be taken care of. Committee chairmen, for example, may announce the next day's hearing schedule, and statements will be prepared for insertion in the *Congressional Record*. In addition, the following day's schedule—as determined by the Majority Leader—will be announced. This will include the time for reconvening, a list of Senators who will be speaking under special orders, the time that routine morning business will end, and the bill to be considered at the conclusion of morning business. It also will include other important items on the schedule, such as agreed-upon recesses for weekly party caucuses or other meetings.

Recess. "Mr. President, I now move that the Senate stand in recess until 9:30 a.m., Tuesday, June 3, 1986." That's the simple form in which the Senate ends its official business for the day—in this case, the historic day that the Senate opened up its Chamber to televised proceedings. By custom, the motion is usually offered by the Majority Leader or his designee. The Senate may also adjourn, but customarily goes into recess instead.

★ 36

THE LEGISLATIVE LABYRINTH

How A Bill Becomes Law

★ ★ ★

Before a bill ever reaches the House or Senate floor, it is put through a series of rigorous tests, each of which may prove an insurmountable barrier. Written comments often are solicited and public hearings held, giving interested parties an opportunity to express opinions about provisions in the legislation. There are subcommittee and full committee votes. There is the matter of scheduling a bill for floor debate. And if a bill makes it that far in the process—and the majority of bills don't—there are intricate parliamentary procedures that opponents can use to prevent its consideration and passage.

It is, in short, a process rife with potential pitfalls, and final approval by one House in no way assures that a bill will be enacted into law, since a similar process will have to be completed by the other body. If the two Houses of Congress disagree over portions of the bill, it may be sent to a conference committee for compromise. So the action a viewer sees in the each Chamber is just one step in a long, exacting process that involves considerable time, energy, and expertise. But the televised action is, in many ways, the make-it-or-break-it point in the life of a bill, and it is at this juncture that the laws of the land are ultimately shaped. Here, then, is a look at how that entire process unfolds.

Introduction and sponsorship. During each two-year Congress, our nation's legislators introduce thousands of new proposals that eventually could become law (the most common form is the bill). The idea for a bill may originate anywhere—with the executive branch, interest groups, corporations, labor unions, congressional committees, or even private citizens, although only Members of Congress, the Resident Commissioner of Puerto Rico, and Delegates from American Samoa, the District of Columbia, Guam, and the Virgin Islands may actually introduce legislation for formal consideration.

In recent history, the President and his administration have been responsible for the bulk of legislative proposals acted on by Congress. Each year, for example, federal departments and agencies submit proposals based on the President's course for the country as outlined in his annual State of the Union message. In addition, the President each year transmits the proposed budget to Congress, which serves as the basis for several appropriations bills drafted by the House Committee on Appropriations after hearings by that committee and its Senate counterpart.

No matter where the legislative proposals originate, though, they follow similar—although by no means exact—paths through Congress. After carefully hammering out specific legislative language, often with the assistance of the Legislative Counsel of the House or Senate, a Member will have the original bill typed on a special form, which includes the names of all those who have signed on as co-sponsors. In the House, the bill is then simply dropped in the hopper beside the House Clerk's desk; in the Senate, Members customarily present bills to the clerks at the Presiding Officer's desk for processing, although Senators occasionally introduce bills from the floor with statements about their content and importance.

The bill's title is subsequently entered in the Journal—each body's official record of its proceedings—and assigned a permanent legislative number—a label often referred to by Members during debate in lieu of the title. A bill originating in the House is designated by the letters "H.R." followed by the assigned

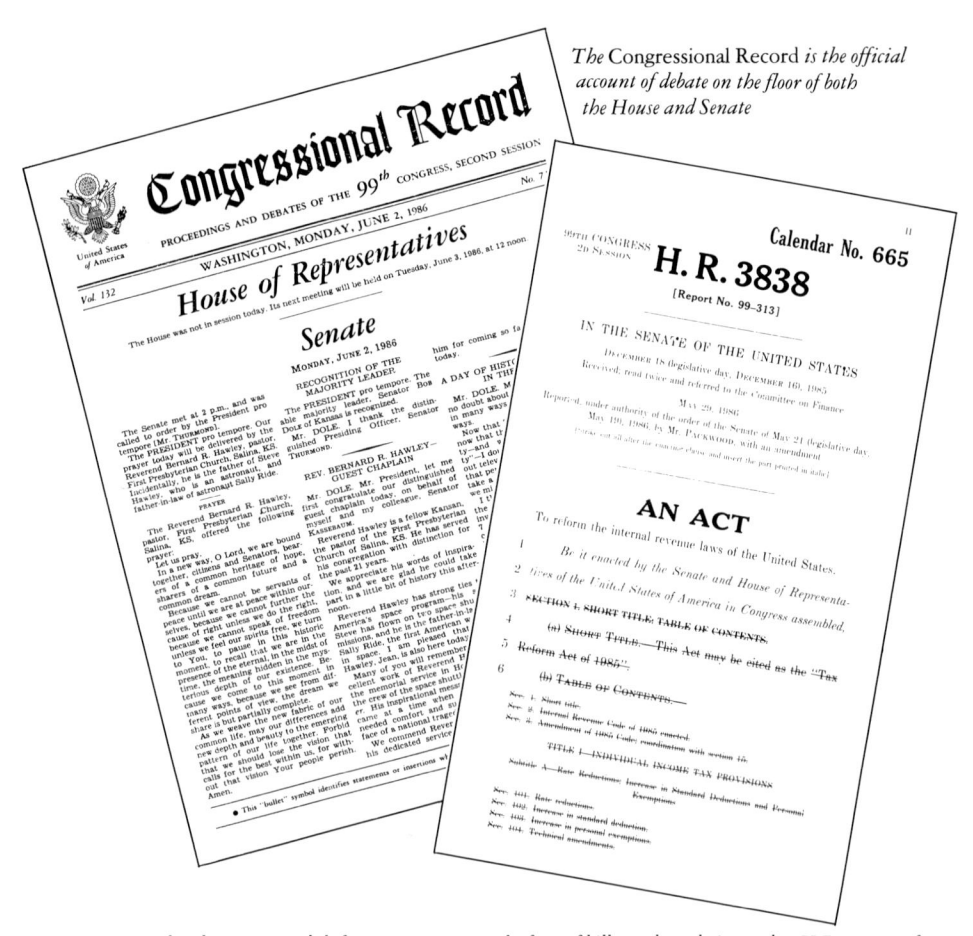

The Congressional Record is the official account of debate on the floor of both the House and Senate

Most legislative proposals before Congress are in the form of bills, and are designated as H.R. (House of Representatives) or S. (Senate) according to the body in which they originate

38

number, while a Senate bill is designated by the letter "S." followed by its number. Numbers are assigned sequentially, in order of introduction, beginning each Congress with number "1."

The next day, the bill appears by title in the *Congressional Record*, along with the name of the committee or committees to which it has been referred—a determination made by the Speaker of the House or, in the Senate, by the Presiding Officer, upon the recommendations of the Parliamentarians. The bill is then sent to the Government Printing Office; shortly thereafter, printed copies are sent to the House and Senate document rooms, where they are made available to Members' offices and the public. In addition, a copy of the bill is sent to the committee to which it has been referred, where it is entered on the committee's Calendar of Business.

Committee action. The committee system is, in effect, the backbone of Congress. It is in committees and subcommittees that bills are closely scrutinized and comments—both from the public and appropriate government agencies—solicited. (There are now 22 permanent "standing" committees in the House and 16 in the Senate. There are also several select committees in each House, which are usually established for a limited period and generally for a strictly limited purpose; and four joint committees, composed of Senators and Representatives, which do not have legislative jurisdiction.) It is here that Members with expertise or interest in a particular subject have an opportunity to advance, modify, or kill a pending piece of legislation. Committee and subcommittee chairmen wield great power. They may decide, for example, to do nothing with a bill, in which case it "dies" at the end of a Congress.

Bills are routinely referred to committees with the appropriate jurisdiction over the subject matter, and then routed to a subcommittee with an even narrower focus. (Some Senate committees have no subcommittees; all work is instead done by the full committees.) A bill proposing to change license requirements for television stations, for example, would be referred to the House Energy and Commerce Committee, and then sent to its Subcommittee on Telecommunications, Consumer Protection and Finance. A similar bill in the Senate would be referred to the Committee on Commerce, Science, and Transportation, and subsequently to the Communications Subcommittee. Here real scrutiny of the bill begins.

The subcommittee staff sometimes solicits comments on the proposal from a wide range of experts: government agencies, affected industries, trade associations, citizen groups, and the like. If the subcommittee's chairman or its members believe the bill deserves an even closer look, and if time allows, public hearings on the bill will be scheduled. Once again, the subcommittee will listen to the views of interested parties—this time in a public forum, with Members given an opportunity to question witnesses. (A committee may go into executive session and close a hearing to the public, but this is usually done only when there is a threat of endangering national security or incriminating a witness.)

When hearings have been completed, a subcommittee will schedule a "mark-up" session to decide whether to move the bill along to the next step in the process: consideration by the full committee. At a mark-up, which also is usually open to the public, Members vote on whether to approve the bill as worded, amend it, rewrite it, or postpone action indefinitely.

HOW A BILL BECOMES LAW

Here's a typical—but greatly simplified—"legislative road map" showing how bills are enacted into law. Most proposals, however, never make it through this legislative labyrinth. In the 98th Congress, for example, of the 9,769 public bills and joint resolutions introduced in both Houses, only 623 (6.4 percent) were enacted into law.

Most legislative proposals are developed by Members of Congress and the executive branch

Introduction

Introduced in House

Introduced in Senate

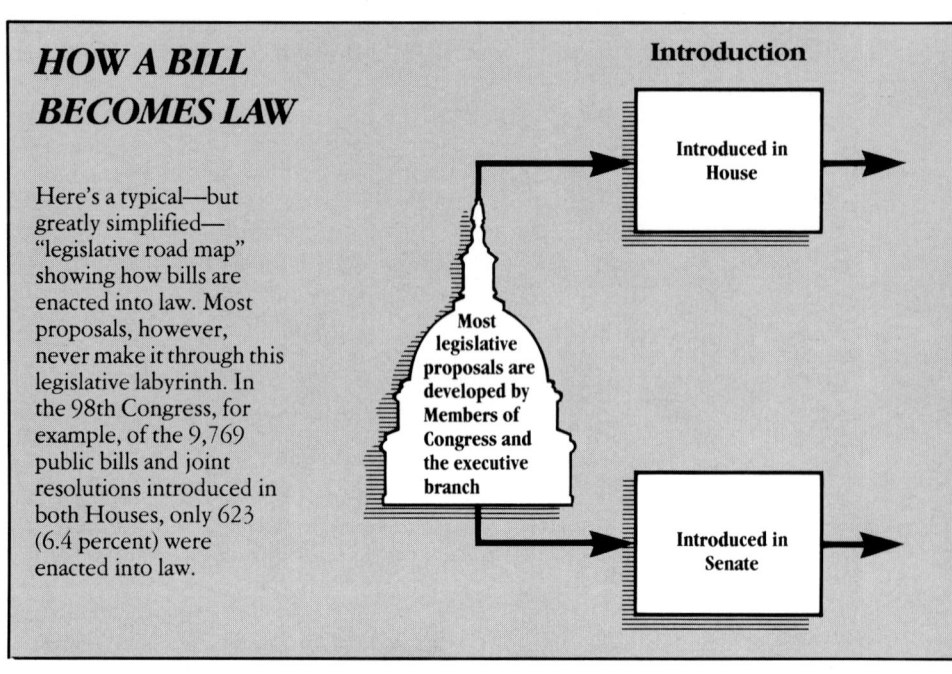

If the bill is sent to the full committee, it may hold its own hearings, or it may proceed to a mark-up and a final vote. The full committee often will review supporting material submitted by the subcommittee, and it may then choose to either table the bill or "report it" to the House or Senate, with or without amendments. Since tabling a bill will ordinarily prevent further action, adverse reports by the full committee are usually considered unnecessary. Occasionally, however, a committee may report a bill unfavorably.

When a committee reports a bill favorably to the full House or Senate, it sends with it a written report describing the purpose of the bill, committee amendments, any minority views, the opinions of other government officials whose views had been solicited, and the committee's reasons for recommended approval. Consequently, these reports form a very important part of the legislative history of the bill, which assumes great significance when courts use it to interpret congressional intent. Like bills, reports are assigned a number, printed, and made available for congressional and public study.

Up to this point, legislation introduced in both Houses of Congress follows similar routes. But this is where the similarities end. The House and Senate procedures for bringing a bill to the floor are entirely different, as are the rules for debate and amending a bill. Here is a description of what happens next in both bodies:

The House

Granting a rule. In large measure, the 13 Members of the House who sit on its powerful Rules Committee determine whether to permit consideration of a par-

Committee Action

After hearings and revisions, full committee may recommend passage

Referred to House committee, then to subcommittee

Referred to Senate committee, then to subcommittee

After hearings and revisions, full committee may recommend passage

Floor Action

House debates, amends, and passes

House and Senate conferees reach compromise

Senate debates, amends, and passes

House must approve compromise

Senate must approve compromise

Enactment Into Law

President signs into law

If President vetoes, Congress may override with two-thirds vote

---

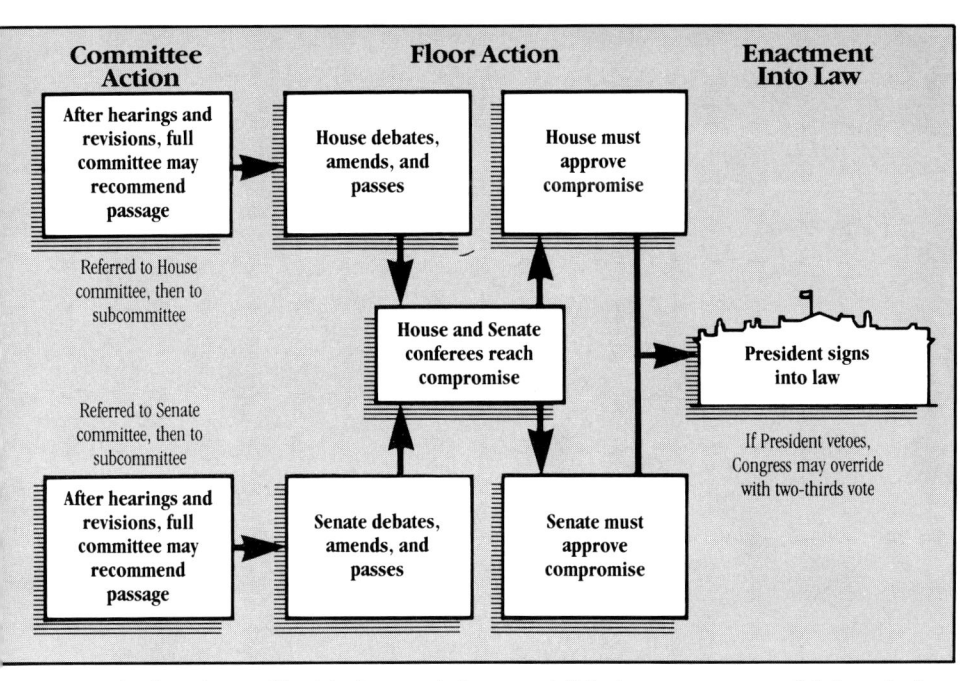

ticular piece of legislation, and then establish the parameters of debate before the bill reaches the floor. Because most controversial pieces of legislation are sent there, the Rules Committee often has been described as the "traffic cop" of the House. (Not all bills require a rule from the Rules Committee to permit consideration, but some require rules to waive points of order against certain provisions.) Following an open hearing (in which the merits of the bill are often discussed), the bill generally will be assigned a debate rule. That rule carefully outlines whether any amendments will be permitted, how long those amendments may be debated, and sometimes even the order in which they may be considered.

It is, without question, a complicated process—but an entirely necessary one in a legislative body with 435 Members. In fact, to keep track of all its pending business (before committees or either Chamber), the House uses five legislative calendars. Under the calendar system, Members sponsoring legislation considered noncontroversial or bills dealing with private matters (claims against the government, immigration, land titles, and the like) may bypass the Rules Committee and gain floor consideration if they have been reported from the committee. Bills on the Consent Calendar, which must be noncontroversial, normally are called on the first and third Mondays of each month; bills on the Private Calendar, the first and third Tuesdays. But if there are sufficient objections, the measure being considered will be postponed or taken off the calendar, and its backers will seek other methods of getting it to the floor. The two basic procedures are a "suspension of the rules" or a special order of the Rules Committee.

Suspension of the Rules. While the term suggests some sort of parliamentary free-for-all, it actually embodies a new set of restrictions for consideration of legislation on the floor. It is a valuable way to expedite consideration of important—but not highly controversial—bills. A motion to suspend the rules is in order on every Monday and Tuesday and during the last six days of every session. Debate is limited to 40 minutes (20 minutes on each side of the issue), and no separate amendments from the floor are permitted. (Committee amendments, however, are often included in the motion, and two-thirds of those present must vote for passage.) If the bill fails, it may be considered later under special order procedures, usually the granting of a rule.

Special orders of the Rules Committee. In essence, the Rules Committee, which functions as an arm of the Speaker, has a range of choices: it may, for example, send a bill to the floor under the normal "open rule," which allows unlimited germane floor amendments debated under the five-minute rule. Among the special rules the committee can provide is a "closed rule," which prohibits all amendments, except perhaps for committee amendments and *pro forma* amendments offered only for purposes of debate. In addition, the committee can propose a variety of other restrictive special rules, which may prohibit or permit only certain amendments. These provisions can be very important, because they can prevent Representatives from offering amendments as alternatives to provisions of the bill, thereby limiting the policy choices that the House can make.

The Rules Committee sets the parameters of how the legislation will be debated once it reaches the floor; the House then debates each special rule and votes to adopt it or reject it. In the event a rule is defeated, the legislation dies. One other parliamentary matter of interest: if a rule is brought to the floor the same day it is reported by the Rules Committee, a two-thirds vote is required for consideration. More often, though, a rule "lies over" at least 24 hours, and only a majority vote is needed for adoption.

The resolution of disagreement over the rule paves the way for a bill to be brought for a vote on the floor. By the time of the final roll-call vote on the rule, many other issues—the rule itself, amendments, the length of time for general debate, and even the manner of voting—will have been decided. The voting process has been greatly streamlined in recent years, but many Members still complain about what they view as an endless string of quorum calls and recorded votes on inconsequential matters.

The Senate

The process by which the Senate brings legislation to the floor differs considerably from that of the House. Here are the specifics:

Scheduling legislative business. When one or more of the Senate's standing committees reports a bill to the Senate floor for debate and passage, the bill is placed on the Senate Calendar of Business—under the heading of "General Orders." The Senate gives its Majority Leader the primary responsibility for deciding the order in which bills on the Calendar should come to the floor for action.

Whenever possible, bills reach the Senate floor not by motion, but by unanimous consent. The motion to consider a bill usually is debatable and, therefore, subject to filibuster. Even before the bill can reach the floor, and perhaps face a filibuster, there may be extended debate on the question of whether or not the Senate should even consider the bill.

It is to avoid this possibility that the Majority Leader attempts to get all Senators to agree by unanimous consent to take up the bill he wishes to have debated. If Senators withhold their consent, they are implicitly threatening extended debate on the question of considering the bill. Senators may do so because they oppose the bill, or because they wish to delay consideration of one measure in the hope of influencing the fate of some other, often unrelated, measure. A single Senator may even place a "hold" on a bill, by which he asks his party's floor leader to object on his behalf to any unanimous consent request to consider the bill—at least until he has been consulted.

In attempting to devise a schedule for the Senate floor, the Majority Leader seeks to promote the legislative program of his party (and perhaps the President, if they are both of the same party), as he also tries to ensure that the Senate considers necessary legislation in a timely fashion. But when he is confronted with two bills, one of which can be brought up by unanimous consent and the other of which cannot, he is naturally inclined to ask the Senate to take up the bill that can be considered without objection. Some bills, of course, are too important to be delayed because some Senators object to considering them. But most are not, especially if the objections can be met through negotiation and compromise. Thus, the possibility of extended debate affects decisions for scheduling legislation in two ways: by discouraging the Majority Leader and the Senate from attempting to take up bills to which some Senators object, and by encouraging negotiations over substantive changes in the bills in order to meet their objections.

Submitting a report. Unlike its House counterpart, the Senate Committee on Rules and Administration does not determine whether legislation should be scheduled for floor debate. At the time a bill is reported by the relevant committee, the Senator making the report may ask unanimous consent for the immediate consideration of the bill. If the bill is noncontroversial and there is no objection, the Senate may pass the measure with little or no debate—and with only a brief explanation of its purpose and effect. Such a procedure does allow for amendments, however, which may be introduced by any Senator. A simple majority vote is required to carry an amendment and pass the bill. If there is any objection, the report must lie over one legislative day and the bill is placed on the calendar.

Call of the Calendar. A bill on the Senate Calendar of business may be called up for action in various ways. It may be called up out of order by unanimous consent, which speeds up Senate business. Large numbers of bills also may be disposed of on call of the Calendar—a special procedure used to consider a number of unobjected to bills and resolutions pending on the calendar. Under this procedure, the proposals are not debated. Furthermore, no Senator may be recognized for more than five minutes on each bill, and no roll-call votes are taken. The bills are merely called up one after another and passed "without objection." Bills remain on the Calendar until disposed of by the Senate, or until the last session of a Congress adjourns *sine die*, which clears out all measures on the calendar.

Time agreements. To avoid endless debate on measures considered by the Senate, complex unanimous consent agreements—often called "time agreements"—are frequently worked out by committee chairmen and party leaders. For example, such agreements may prohibit the introduction of non-germane amendments, they may limit the number of Senators permitted to speak on each question, or they may put a strict limitation on the time available for debating the bill and every question that may arise during its consideration. Such agreements cannot be imposed on the Senate by any vote of that body, but rather require the concurrence of every Member. Any Senator who is dissatisfied with the terms of a proposed time agreement has only to object, and the standing rules remain in force. As a result, time agreements often include exceptions to their general provisions in order to satisfy individual Senators.

The Senate often begins consideration of bills without having reached a time limitation agreement. In some cases, the floor managers expect few amendments and relatively little debate, making an elaborate agreement unnecessary. In other cases, the Majority Leader and committee chairman seek an agreement unsuccessfully, but proceed with the bill anyway because of its timeliness and importance. After the Senate has debated such a bill and controversial amendments—perhaps for days—the leaders often renew their attempts to reach an overall agreement limiting debate on each amendment, or an agreement setting a time for the Senate to vote on whether to pass the bill. If no such overall agreement can be reached, they often try to arrange unanimous consent agreements for more limited purposes while the Senate is debating a bill—time limits on individual amendments, temporarily setting aside one amendment to consider another, and so on.

The amending process is at the heart of the Senate's floor deliberations, and such agreements over amendments pave the way for a final vote on a bill. In fact, if the Senate reaches a final vote on passing or defeating a bill, the bill is very likely to pass.

Further Action

Once a bill passes the House or Senate, it is transmitted to the other Chamber in a rather formal ceremony (similar to the procedure under which messages are delivered from the President). There it follows a similarly labyrinthine path to final deliberations. (After the passage of a bill by one body, it technically becomes an "act"—not yet effective as a law—but it nevertheless continues to be generally referred to as a bill.)

If a bill or resolution originates in the Senate, following passage it is messaged to the House and referred to a House committee; the committee reports it to the House and it is acted on by that body. If amended, it is returned to the Senate for concurrence in the House amendments. A bill or resolution originating in the House follows the same steps, except in reverse.

A bill cannot become the law of the land until it has been approved in identical terms by both Houses of Congress. So if there are differences between the

The House Rules Committee decides how and even if legislation will be debated.

House and Senate versions when each body completes its deliberations, they may seek to work them out in conference (see the following section). Each body appoints conferees, usually drawn from the committee involved in the legislation. They meet and try to resolve disagreements. If they are unable to do so, new conferees may be chosen in an attempt to break the deadlock.

Once approved, the conference committee's report, which represents all amendments between the Houses on which the conferees could agree, is sent back to each House for consideration.

After the House and Senate have passed a bill in exactly the same language, it is printed on parchment and transmitted to the President for his signature. The President may approve the bill simply by signing it, or he may veto it. If Congress is in session and the President does not veto the measure within 10 days and return it with his objections, the Constitution provides that it become law anyway. If, however, Congress has adjourned *sine die* and the President fails to sign a bill, it is known as a "pocket veto." (In essence, Congress has prevented the bill's return by virtue of its adjournment.)

If the President vetoes the bill, it is sent back to the House of origin with a message explaining why (the "veto message"). A vetoed bill is privileged, and generally is voted on at once—unless the vote is postponed or the bill is referred to committee, which normally kills the bill. If two-thirds of the House to which the vetoed bill has been sent agree to pass the bill, it is then sent to the other House. A two-thirds affirmative vote in that body is then required to override a presidential veto. Failure of either House to override sustains the veto.

CONFERENCE COMMITTEES

"The Third House of Congress"

★ ★ ★

Because of its critical role in the legislative process, the conference committee is often referred to as the "Third House of Congress."

The Constitution mandates that a bill cannot become the law of the land until it has been approved in identical terms by both Houses. If there are differences between a House and Senate bill when each body completes its deliberations, a conference committee may be called to hammer out an acceptable compromise.

The conferees, known as "managers," are appointed by the Speaker of the House and, in the Senate, by unanimous consent by the Presiding Officer. Typically, a conference committee will have seven or eight Members from each body, representing both parties, all of whom will have had some responsibility for the legislation. Either House may appoint a larger number of conferees, but, because the conferees of each House vote as a unit, that does not offer any advantage. Whatever the size of the conference committee, though, a majority from each delegation must be from that body's majority party.

The meetings of the conferees are customarily held on the Senate side of the Capitol, and, unless a special vote is taken, are open to the public—including TV cameras.

The conferees are strictly limited in their consideration to matters in disagreement between the two Houses. In addition, conferees may be instructed, by a vote in Chamber, as to the position they are to take. Conferees technically are not bound by these instructions, but they are an indication of the sense of their body, and therefore they likely will pay attention to them.

After deliberations, which generally include intense negotiations, each side hoping to prevail in its positions, they may make one or more recommendations when reporting back to their respective bodies. For example, they may recommend that the House withdraw all or certain of its amendments, or that the Senate withdraw its disagreement to all or certain of the House amendments. Or they may report an inability to agree—in total or in part. Usually there is a compromise, but if no agreement can be reached, new conferees may be appointed in either or both Houses.

When the conferees, by a majority vote of each side, reach complete agreement (or agreement on some, but not all, amendments) they incorporate their recommendations in a report, written by the conference committee staff. Iden-

Like bills, reports are numbered and printed

tical reports are filed in each House, along with a detailed and explicit statement informing Congress of the effect that the conferees' amendments or propositions will have on the original measure.

The conference report is not subject to amendment, and, following debate, generally must be accepted or rejected in its entirety. The House may vote separately, however, on amendments proposed by the Senate that may not be germane to the House-passed bill. If they don't agree on these amendments, the conference report is then rejected and a new conference may be convened, or the Senate may accept that portion of the House conference report rejected by the separate vote of the House.

House rules require that conference reports "lie over" at least three days to ensure that Members have time to study them before they vote. The House generally permits one hour of floor debate on the conference report itself; if any amendments are considered separately, they must be sent back to the Senate for approval or further conference. The Senate may act immediately on a conference report; if the time for debate on the adoption of the report is limited, the time allotted must be equally divided between the majority and minority parties.

If a conference report is rejected by either House, it so notifies the other body and usually requests another conference; however, it may merely notify the second body of its action without requesting a further conference, leaving further steps to be taken by the other House.

When the bill—either with or without amendments—has been agreed to in identical form by both Houses, it is delivered to the enrolling clerk of the House in which it originated. Along with the original "engrossed" bill—the bill as it passed the House in which it was introduced—the enrolling clerk receives the conference report, amendments, and all other pertinent papers. The enrolled bill, reflecting all changes adopted by both Houses, is then printed on parchment paper, signed by the Speaker of the House and then the President of the Senate, and delivered to the White House. The President may then approve the bill or veto it.

THE AYES HAVE IT

How Members of Congress Vote

★ ★ ★

Voting, quite simply, is the process by which actions are completed in Congress. For a bill to become law, both Houses must vote affirmatively, followed, of course, by presidential approval. Parliamentary procedure allows for various types of votes, and a series of preliminary votes usually occurs before a measure is approved or rejected.

Viewers of House and Senate floor action will quickly recognize one major difference in voting procedures: the House, unlike the Senate, uses an electronic voting system. This innovation is a relatively recent one, dating back to January 23, 1973. Before that, tallying Members' positions on legislation was a time-consuming process, as roll-call votes—which required reading each Representative's name aloud—took 30-40 minutes or so to complete. But with the introduction of the electronic vote, which uses a sophisticated computer system, the process was simplified and streamlined. Now, in fact, an electronic vote is usually completed in 15 minutes.

Each Member of the House is issued a coded identification card—about the size of a credit card—that is placed into any of 44 voting stations around the Chamber when a vote has been ordered. A blue light signifies to Members that the station is available for use; when the card is inserted in the machine, and the computer determines that it is valid, a Member then pushes the proper button—which lights up when depressed—to signify his intended vote: yea (green), nay (red), or present (amber).

To keep track of how the vote is proceeding, electronic scoreboards have been placed in strategic spots in the House Chamber. On each side of the Chamber, for example, display panels summarize the bill under consideration, the time left to vote, and a running tally of how Members have voted. In addition, four display panels, which include all House Members, are located on the wall above and behind the Speaker's rostrum. When a Member casts his vote at a voting station, a corresponding light next to his name—indicating how he has voted—is illuminated.

Five video display consoles, which offer information and pertinent statistics about the vote, are also located in the Chamber. Two consoles, available for Members' use, are positioned in the rear of the Chamber; consoles are also found at the Majority and Minority Leaders' tables. The remaining console—the control console used to oversee the electronic voting process—is at the Tally Clerk's desk. The actual computers recording and compiling the voting information are in the Rayburn House Office Building. Should one computer fail, a backup takes over and keeps the system operating.

House Members place a coded identification card into consoles in the Chamber and then register their votes

Under House rules, Members may change their votes by reinserting their cards in any of the voting stations during the first 10 minutes of a 15-minute vote. In the last five minutes they must submit a tally card at the desk. Once a vote has been completed, the scoreboard lights are dimmed, the Clerk announces the results, and the House moves on to other business.

Here are the four types of votes used in the House:

Recorded Vote or **Yea-and-Nay Vote**. A recorded vote may be ordered by one-fifth of a quorum (44 in a full House, and 20 in the Committee of the Whole), while the yeas-and-nays may be ordered by one-fifth of those present. These roll-call votes require Members to vote yea, nay, or present. Although the Speaker may order that the roll be read, with Members responding in turn, the electronic voting system is used almost exclusively.

Voice Vote. This method of voting does not rely on actual totals of pro or con votes. Instead, Members answer "aye" or "nay" in chorus, and the presiding officer decides which side prevailed.

Standing Vote. If the result of a voice vote is uncertain, a standing vote (or "division vote") may be taken on demand of any Member. For a standing vote, the actual numerical results of which also are not recorded, Members in favor of a proposal stand and are counted; then, Members opposed stand and are counted.

★★★★★

Thomas Edison first suggested the idea of electronic voting for Congress in 1912, but it wasn't until January 1973 that the current electronic voting system in the House was put into use.

Teller Vote. In this method of voting, which generally has been replaced by the electronic voting system, Members walk up the center aisle past two "tellers," who keep count as the legislators pass. The ayes walk first past the tellers, followed by the nays. A teller vote can only be ordered upon demand of one-fifth of a quorum: 44 in the House, and 20 in the Committee of the Whole.

Unlike the House, the Senate has no electronic voting system, nor does it use the teller vote. But like the House, the Senate uses voice, division, and roll-call votes.

The voice vote is the most commonly used alternative to the roll-call vote, and the procedure in the Senate mirrors that in the House: Senators answer "yea" or "nay" in chorus, and the presiding officer determines the outcome. The division vote is a less likely alternative to the roll-call vote, but it too is conducted in similar fashion to the House procedure, with Senators rising to indicate their position on a vote. Although neither of these methods of voting creates a public record of how each Senator voted, they are nonetheless valid and conclusive ways for the Senate to reach a decision.

Most roll-call votes occur on amendments, and can be ordered by one-fifth of the Senators on the floor—assuming a quorum is present. Since the smallest possible quorum is 51 Senators, the support of at least 11 Senators is required to order a roll-call vote. If a quorum is not present, a Senator may suggest the absence of a quorum, at which time the Legislative Clerk summons Senators to the floor and begins to call the roll.

A Senator who has been recognized can ask for "the yeas-and-nays" at any time that the Senate is considering a bill, amendment, motion, or other question. If the roll call is ordered, that is how the Senate will vote on the question whenever the time for the vote arrives. Thus, the Senate may order a roll-call vote on an amendment when it is offered, but the actual vote, which will follow debate, may not take place for several hours or more.

Sen. John Breaux (D-La.). Written descriptions appear across the bottom of the TV screen explaining debates and votes taking place.

The length of time for roll-call votes is established by the Senate at the start of each Congress. When the 99th Congress convened, on January 3, 1985, the Senate agreed there would be a limitation of 15 minutes each on any roll-call vote; that is typical of previous sessions of Congress. On occasion, unanimous consent is obtained limiting a vote to 10 minutes. Ten-minute votes are usually desired in an effort to conserve time when a succession of two or more (back-to-back) votes is ordered, the first taking 15 minutes and those following 10 minutes each.

Because voting is such a crucial part of the legislative process, voting times are routinely arranged to accommodate Senators. In addition, party leaders give their colleagues advance notice about upcoming key votes. If you follow Senate debate closely, you will hear agreements being worked out about the scheduling of votes on amendments, as well as the time for a final vote on a bill.

When a roll-call vote is ordered, the Legislative Clerk begins reading the roll of the Senate in alphabetical order. During these procedures, television viewers see a wide-angle view of the Chamber; from time to time you'll also see the Legislative Clerk, superimposed in a circle, reading the roll.

When an electronic vote is conducted in the House, a running tally is displayed on your TV screen. When a Senate roll-call vote is conducted, however, no such information is displayed. When the vote has been completed, the Legislative Clerk announces the final tally; the yea and nay totals are then displayed for TV viewers.

A Post-TV Guide

Where To Go for More Information

★ ★ ★

Watching the proceedings of Congress may be the purest form of educational television, but the education doesn't have to end after you've turned off the TV set. Something you see on the screen, in fact, may be the starting point for taking advantage of Capitol Hill's vast resources in providing information and assistance. Here are a few ways to follow up:

Congressional Record. Published every day Congress is in session, the *Congressional Record* is the official account of debate on the floor of both the House and Senate. That account, however, may sometimes differ from what you've seen on the screen, because Members of Congress are allowed to edit their remarks before publication. Material inserted in the *Record* but not actually presented on the floor appears in smaller type; insertions of entire statements gen-

★ ★ ★ ★ ★

On October 17, 1940, four-month-old Robert J. Coar, Jr., whose father was superintendent of the House Radio Transcription Room, was christened in the well of the House. Following the ceremony, the House passed a rule that it could not be done again.

erally are marked by bullets (●). The *Record*'s "Daily Digest" highlights both floor and committee actions, and lists committee meetings scheduled for the next day.

Most major libraries subscribe to the *Congressional Record*. Single copies may be obtained by sending a check or money order for $1 to: Superintendent of Documents, Government Printing Office, Washington, D.C. 20402.

Congressional documents. For free copies of House and Senate documents—including bills, resolutions, presidential messages to Congress, most committee reports, and public laws—write:

Senate Document Room
Hart Senate Office Building, Room B-04
Washington, D.C. 20510
(202) 224-7860

★ 52

Under rules established by Congress in June 1986, members of the general public may obtain up to six free items per inquiry; there are modest fees for each additional item requested. You may wish to telephone first to check on availability and, if ordering a number of documents, possible charges.

A special sales office has been established at the U.S. Government Printing Office for the sale of committee prints and hearings. To place an order by mail, write:

Superintendent of Documents
Congressional Sales Office—Main GPO
Washington, D.C. 20402-9315

★ ★ ★ ★ ★

On June 8, 1977, the Senate Subcommittee on Science, Technology and Space, meeting in Washington, D.C., conducted a hearing via satellite with witnesses in Springfield, Illinois. The closed-circuit session marked the first time the Senate conducted a hearing via satellite videoconference.

For information about the publications this office has for sale, along with prices, phone (202) 275-3030. A telephone recording with information on the newest committee prints and hearings available for sale can be reached by calling (202) 512-2424.

Status of legislation. For information on the status of legislation in either the House or Senate (whether there have been committee hearings, dates of upcoming hearings, the number of committee reports, and so forth), contact: Bill Status Office, 2nd and D Streets SW, Room 696, Washington, D.C. 20515. Telephone: (202) 225-1772.

Floor action. In both the House and Senate, each party's cloakroom maintains recorded messages that give callers running accounts of what is happening (or has just happened) on the floor. Here are the cloakroom numbers:

House: (202) 225-7400 (Democratic)
(202) 225-7430 (Republican)
Senate: (202) 224-8541 (Democratic)
(202) 224-8601 (Republican)

Members of Congress. Your Representative and Senators will be happy to provide you with similar information about pending legislation or other congressional matters in which you may be interested. Their office addresses are included in most issues of the *Congressional Record*, as well as in standard reference books like the *Congressional Directory* and *Congressional Staff Directory*. The Capitol Hill switchboard, at (202) 224-3121, can connect you with the office of any Member of Congress, committee, or subcommittee.

READING GUIDE

Keeping Tabs on Capitol Hill

★ ★ ★

Congressional Picture Directory. This paperback guide is a useful companion for watching the televised proceedings of Congress; it may help you identify Members milling about on the floor or waiting to speak. For information, write: Superintendent of Documents, Government Printing Office, Washington, D.C. 20402.

Congressional Directory. The *Congressional Directory* gives biographies of each member of Congress, committee assignments, maps of the nation's 435 congressional districts, and much more—including a listing of all federal departments and agencies, with addresses, telephone numbers, and titles of officials. Senators and Representatives are listed by state, in alphabetical order by name, and by term of service. For information, write: Superintendent of Documents, Government Printing Office, Washington, D.C. 20402.

The Almanac of American Politics (by Michael Barone and Grant Ujifusa) and **Politics in America** (Alan Ehrenhalt, editor). These reference books contain profiles of each Senator, Representative, and Governor, voting records on key issues, ratings by special interest groups, and in-depth analyses of each state and congressional district. Both books are available at most libraries and bookstores.

Congressional Quarterly Weekly Report and **National Journal.** CQ's *Weekly Report* probably is the best running account of what goes on in Congress. If you're interested in a quick overview of an issue before Congress, or an individual's voting record, this is the place to start. *National Journal* is a weekly periodical that reports and analyzes important executive branch and congressional actions. Both publications are available in most major libraries.

The U.S. Congress Handbook. This annual guide to Congress includes Members' pictures, biographies, and committee assignments, as well as information on Cabinet officers. Single copies are $9.95, available from C-SPAN Publications, 1616 Main Street, Lynchburg, VA 24504-1913.

CIS Index. Since 1970, Congressional Information Service (a private research firm located in Bethesda, Maryland, just outside of Washington, D.C.) has indexed summaries of hearings, reports, documents, committee prints, and other congressional publications. The information is arranged by committee. Indexes are by subject, name, witness, title, bill number, report and document numbers, and, in the annual volume, by the public law number. Many major libraries have the quarterly and annual volumes; some subscribe to CIS's weekly looseleaf service.

LEGISLATIVE LEXICON
A Glossary of Key Congressional Terms

★ ★ ★

Act. Legislation that has passed both Houses of Congress and has been signed by the President or passed over his veto, thus becoming law. An act also is a bill or joint resolution passed and engrossed by either House.

Adjournment Motion. A motion of the highest privilege, which is not debated, that allows each House to adjourn each day. To adjourn from day to day does not require a quorum, but to adjourn to a day certain does, if demanded.

Adjournment to a Day Certain. Adjournment under a motion or concurrent resolution which fixes the next time of meeting. Neither House may adjourn for more than three days without consent of the other. A session of Congress is not ended by adjournment to a day certain.

Adjournment Sine Die. Adjournment without setting a definite date for reconvening, it usually signifies the final adjournment of a session of Congress. A new session usually begins on January 3 and can continue until January 3 of the following year, but the convening date may be changed by majority vote of both Houses, enacted into law.

Administration Bill. An informal designation indicating that the bill is part of the President's program.

Amendment. Proposal of a Member to alter the language or stipulations in a bill or act. It is voted on in the same manner as a bill.

Appropriation Bill. Grants the actual money usually approved by authorization bills, but not necessarily the total amount permissible. An appropriation bill originates in the House, and normally is not acted on until its authorization measure is enacted.

Authorization Bill. Authorizes a program, specifies its general aim and conduct, and, unless "open-ended," puts a ceiling on monies that can be used to finance it. Usually enacted before the related appropriation bill, which actually makes money available, is passed.

Bills. Most legislative proposals before Congress are in the form of bills, and are designated as H.R. (House of Representatives) or S. (Senate) according to the body in which they originate and by a number assigned in the order in which they were introduced, from the beginning of each two-year congressional term. "Public bills" deal with general questions, and become Public Laws if approved by Congress and signed by the President. Any number of Members may join in introducing a single bill. "Private bills," introduced with declining frequency in recent years, deal with individual matters such as claims against the government, immigration and naturalization cases, land titles, and the like, and become Private Laws if approved and signed.

Bills Referred. When introduced, a bill is referred to the committee (or committees) having jurisdiction over the subject covered by the bill. Bills are referred by the Speaker of the House and the Presiding Officer in the Senate on advice of the Parliamentarian, according to House and Senate rules. In the House, committees may appeal these decisions.

By Request. Measures can be submitted with the phrase "by request," a term found on bills and resolutions introduced or submitted at the request of the Administration or private organizations or individuals, following the name of the sponsor. Such proposals, though introduced as a courtesy, are not necessarily favored by the Members sponsoring them.

★ ★ ★

Calendar. An agenda of pending business before committees or either Chamber.

Chamber. Meeting place for the total membership of either the House or Senate, as distinguished from the respective committee rooms.

Cloture. A method by which filibuster can be ended in the Senate. In most cases, a filibuster may be limited if a cloture motion, signed by 16 Senators, is agreed to by at least three-fifths of all Senators. After cloture is invoked, there are 30 hours for debate, roll calls, quorum calls, and other procedural matters. The Senate then votes on all questions still pending, followed by a final vote on the bill.

Companion Bill. A bill introduced in one House, often identical to legislation submitted in the other.

Concurrent Resolution. Designated H. Con. Res. or S. Con Res., it must be adopted by both Houses but does not require the signature of the President. A concurrent resolution does not have the force of law; instead, it generally is used to make or amend rules applicable to both Houses, or to express the sentiment of the two Houses. For example, it might be used to convey the congratulations of Congress to another country on the anniversary of its independence, or fix time for adjournment of Congress.

Conference. A meeting between committee members ("conferees") of the House and Senate to reconcile differences over provisions of a bill.

Congressional Record. The transcript of debate and proceedings in both the House and Senate Chambers, printed daily when Congress is in session.

Consent Calendar. Noncontroversial reported bills may be placed on the Consent Calendar and brought up on the first and third Mondays of each month in the House of Representatives. Objection by three or more Members will strike the bill from the Consent Calendar. A bill also may be passed over without prejudice to a later date. A bill killed on the Consent Calendar may still be brought to the floor under other procedures.

Continuing Resolution. When a fiscal year ends without an approved appropriation for each executive department or agency for the following fiscal year, a continuing resolution is enacted allowing departments to spend at a specified rate—usually the previous year's spending level.

★ ★ ★

Discharge a Committee. Relieve a committee from jurisdiction over a measure before it that has not been reported.

Discharge Motion. A parliamentary procedure in the House that discharges a committee from considering a bill. If a petition is signed by a majority of all House Members (218) and the motion is then passed by a majority, the bill is brought to the floor for consideration without being reported by the committee.

★ ★ ★

Enacting Clause. A legally required phrase at the beginning of all bills and resolutions, without which legislation could not be enacted. The clause reads: "Be it enacted by the Senate and House of Representatives assembled" .... If adopted, a motion to strike the enacting clause kills the bill.

Engrossed Bill. The final copy of a bill as passed by one House, with all the amendments agreed to by Members, and certified by the Clerk of the House or the Secretary of the Senate. At this point the measure technically becomes an act (not yet effective as a law), but it nonetheless continues to be generally referred to as a bill.

Enrolled Bill. The precise, final bill as passed in identical form by both Houses of Congress. The enrolled bill is printed on parchment and signed by an officer of the House of origin (House Clerk or Senate Secretary). It is then examined for accuracy by officials of the House in which it originated, and finally sent on for signatures of the House Speaker, the Senate President, and the President of the United States.

Executive Calendar. Published by the Executive Clerk, this non-legislative calendar lists presidential documents, such as nominations and treaties, which have been reported by committees and are pending action by the Senate as a whole.

Executive Communications. Messages from the President and executive agencies to the Speaker of the House and the President of the Senate, usually requesting legislation, making a report, or expressing a view on problems and policies.

Executive Session. A meeting of a congressional committee—or even the entire Chamber—that can be attended only by the group's members or those invited: an expert witness, for example, or other Members of Congress. This should not be confused with another, more specific term: Executive Session of the Senate. The executive business of the Senate includes both nominations and treaties submitted to Congress by the President for that Chamber's advice and consent. Such executive business is handled differently than legislative business; for one thing, there is a separate Executive Calendar. When an Executive Session of the Senate is held, that body meets—either in open or closed session—to consider business on this Executive Calendar.

★ ★ ★

Filibuster. A time-honored Senate tradition, the filibuster is a way of balancing minority rights with the principle of rule by the majority. By threatening unlimited debate, a Senator or group of Senators can force the majority to amend or even abandon a particular piece of legislation. A filibuster can last for many days, and is a tactic of last resort for a determined minority. By invoking cloture (see above), a procedure under Senate rules, a filibuster can be halted.

Fiscal Year. The government's bookkeeping year, which runs from October 1 to September 30 of the following year. The date of the fiscal year is designated by the calendar year in which it ends. For example, fiscal year 1985, often written FY85, began October 1, 1984 and ended September 30, 1985.

Floor. Literally, the floor of the Chamber in which the House or Senate meets. Figuratively, the term refers to the place in which matters are considered by the full House or Senate.

Floor Manager. A Member, usually representing sponsors of a bill, responsible for trying to steer a piece of legislation through floor debate and amendment to passage. A floor manager is often the chairman of the full committee or subcommittee that reported the bill. In this role, he is responsible for allocating the time granted supporters of the bill for debate. The minority leader or the ranking minority member of the committee often apportions time for the minority party's participation in the debate, even if he favors the legislation.

★ ★ ★

Germane. Pertaining to the subject matter of the measure at hand. All House amendments must be germane to the bill or to the amendment to which offered, and a non-germane amendment can be stricken with a point of order. The Senate requires that amendments be germane only when they are being considered under cloture, or, often, when proceeding under an agreement to limit debate.

★ ★ ★

House. The familiar term for the House of Representatives, as distinct from the Senate; each body, however, is a "House" of Congress.

House Calendar. A listing of public bills, other than direct or indirect appropriations or revenue measures, reported from committee and awaiting action by the House of Representatives.

★ ★ ★

Joint Meeting of Congress. A ceremonial occasion when both Houses recess and meet together, distinguished from a joint session in that business is not in order. Since only the President may address a joint session, other dignitaries, on ceremonial occasions such as State visits, may address a joint meeting of Congress.

Joint Resolution. Designated by H.J. Res. or S.J. Res., it requires the approval of both Houses and (with one exception) the signature of the President, and has the force of law if approved. There is no real difference between a bill and joint resolution. Joint resolutions also are used to propose amendments to the Constitution, but do not require presidential signatures; they become part of the Constitution when ratified by three-fourths of the states.

Joint Session. An occasion upon which both Houses of Congress meet together (traditionally in the House Chamber) to receive a message from the President or count electoral ballots. Joint sessions are considered business sessions of Congress, as distinguished from the ceremonial joint meetings.

★ ★ ★

Lame Duck Session. A session of Congress, called after a general congressional election between November and January 3, that includes Members who have been defeated or are returning.

Law. (see *Act*)

Legislative Day. The period of time from the meeting of either House following an adjournment until its next adjournment. The House usually adjourns from day to day, so legislative days and calendar days usually coincide. But the legislative day in the Senate often runs for many calendar days, as the Senate often recesses—rather than adjourns—from day to day.

★ ★ ★

Majority Leader. The chief strategist and floor spokesman for the majority party in the House or Senate. He is elected by his party colleagues meeting in caucus or conference.

Majority Whip. The assistant leader in the House or Senate. His job is to help keep track of all important political legislation and try to have party members present when key measures are to be voted on.

Marking Up a Bill. Going through a measure, in committee or subcommittee, section by section—revising language, adding amendments, and so forth. If the measure is extensively revised, the new version may be introduced as a separate bill, with a new number.

Minority Leader. Floor leader for the minority party. (see *Majority Leader*)

Minority Whip. Peforms duties of the whip for the minority party. (see *Majority Whip*)

Motion. A formal proposal, often presented in writing, on which a vote must be taken in the affirmative in order to move it forward.

★ ★ ★

Notice Quorum Call. In the Committee of the Whole, a notice quorum call may be ordered by the Chairman when a point of order is made that a quorum is not present. If 100 House Members—who constitute a quorum in the Committee of the Whole—appear within the specified time period, the notice quorum call is not recorded. If 100 Members fail to appear, a regular quorum call, which is recorded, is made.

★ ★ ★

Override a Veto. If the President disapproves a bill and sends it back to Congress with his objections, Congress may override his veto by a two-thirds vote in each Chamber. The Constitution requires a yea-and-nay vote.

★ ★ ★

Parliamentarian. The rules expert charged with advising the presiding officer on questions of procedure.

Parliamentary Inquiry. A question from a Member to the chair seeking clarification on a procedural matter. A Member who holds the floor may yield for that purpose and the chair will render an opinion.

Point of Order. In effect, an objection raised by a Member that the pending proceedings are in violation of some rule of the Chamber and, at the same time, a demand for immediate return to the regular order.

President of the Senate. The Constitution designates the Vice President of the United States as the presiding officer of the Senate. Normally, the Vice President only presides over the Senate if an upcoming vote is expected to be close, because he can vote to break a tie. In his absence, the President *pro tempore* (president for the time being) presides.

President Pro Tempore. The President *pro tempore* (also known as president *pro tem*) is responsible for presiding over the Senate in the absence of the Vice President; he also oversees the day-to-day operations of the Senate. The President *pro tem* is elected by his fellow Senators. Traditionally, the Senator of the majority party with the longest continuous service is elected.

Presiding Officer. Any Member of the Senate designated by the President *pro tempore* to preside during Senate sessions. Customarily, majority party Members preside, normally for one hour at a time.

Previous Question. In this sense, a "question" is an "issue" before the House for a vote, and the issue is "previous" when some other topic has superseded it in the attention of the Chamber. A motion for the previous question, when carried, has the effect of cutting off all debate and amendments and forcing a vote on the subject originally at hand. If, however, the previous question is moved and carried before there has been any debate on the subject at hand, and the subject is debatable, 40 minutes of debate is allowed before the vote. The previous question is sometimes moved to prevent amendments from being introduced and voted on.

Private Calendar. Private House bills dealing with individual matters such as claims against the government, immigration, and land titles are put on this calendar. Two Members may block consideration of a private bill in the Chamber. If blocked, it is then recommitted to committee.

Privileged Question. Privileged questions are issues which the rules of each House give special priority over other items of business. It is a general rule in Congress, for example, that the question first moved and seconded shall be voted on first. But this rule gives way to what may be called privileged questions, which may temporarily supersede a pending question or require recognition by the chair. This is to be distinguished from a preferential motion. A motion to refer, for instance, may, under certain circumstances, be superseded by a motion to table, and a vote would be forced on the latter motion only. But a motion to adjourn takes precedence over all others, and is thus considered the "highest privilege."

★ ★ ★

Questions of Privilege. These are matters addressable by resolution affecting the rights of Congress collectively—its safety, dignity, and the integrity of its proceedings, including such matters as admission to the floor, the conduct of officers and employees, and the unauthorized release of information to the media; it also includes the rights, reputation, and conduct of individual Members in their representative capacity. Questions of "personal privilege" relate to individual Members of Congress. A Member's rising to a question of personal privilege is given precedence over almost all other proceedings, except questions of privilege of the House.

Quorum. The number of Members required for the transaction of business. In the Senate and House, it is a simple majority of the membership (when there are no vacancies, 51 in the Senate and 218 in the House). A quorum is 100 in the Committee of the Whole House. Failure to achieve a quorum is cause for adjournment.

★ ★ ★

Recess. Each House may find it necessary to suspend its business for short or indefinite periods of time during a legislative day. Unlike adjournment, a recess does not end a legislative day and, as such, does not interfere with unfinished business. The House usually adjourns from day to day. The Senate often recesses from day to day rather than adjourn, so that a legislative day may encompass several calendar days.

Recommit to Committee. A motion to send a bill back to the committee that reported it. Generally speaking, a motion to recommit, if adopted, means the end of floor consideration of the bill unless the motion is accompanied by instructions to report back "forthwith."

Recommit to Committee with Instructions. A motion to send a bill back to the committee that reported it, with specific instructions to report it back to the floor "forthwith"—usually within a specified time period and with certain modifications, amendments, deletions, and so forth.

Reconsider a Vote. Each body has procedures for reconsidering votes that it takes. Under the rules of each House, no vote is in itself conclusive until a motion to reconsider has been disposed of. In the House it may be made only by a Member who voted on the prevailing side of the original question, and must be entered either on the same day or on the next succeeding day the House is in session. In the Senate the motion may be made only by a Member who voted on the prevailing side of the question or by a Member who did not vote at all.

Report. A "report" is the document setting forth the committee's explanation of its action. House and Senate reports are numbered separately and designated S. Rept. or H. Rept. Conference reports are numbered and designated in the same way as regular committee reports.

Most reports favor a bill's passage. Adverse reports are occasionally submitted, but more often, when a committee disapproves a bill, it simply fails to "report" it at all to the full House or Senate. When a committee report is not unanimous, the dissenting committee members may file a statement of their views, which is referred to as a minority report. Members also may file "supplemental" or "additional" views. Sometimes a bill is reported without recommendation.

Reporting a Rule. (see *Rule*)

Resolutions. Simple resolutions, designated by H. Res. or S. Res., deal with matters entirely within the prerogatives of either the House or Senate, and require neither passage by the other Chamber nor approval by the President. They do not have the force of law, and most deal with the rules or sense of one House. (see *Concurrent Resolution, Joint Resolution*)

Rule. The term has two different congressional meanings. The Constitution provides that each House may determine the rules of its proceedings—the order in which it considers legislation, for example, voting procedures, duties of its officers, and so forth. These are all stipulated in the Chamber's book of rules.

A second meaning is specific to the House of Representatives. The House Rules Committee not only makes recommendations to the House on its rules, but also makes recommendations to the House on the handling of a particular bill on the floor. The committee affects the order of business by reporting resolutions that make it possible for the body to begin acting on a bill on the House or Union Calendar. These resolutions are known as special orders or simply as "rules."

Each special rule also proposes a set of ground rules for debating and amending a particular bill. For example, a special rule may impose limitations on the amendments that Members can propose to a bill, or it may allow an amendment to be offered that violates a standing rule of the House. The House as a whole decides by majority vote whether to accept, reject, or modify each special rule proposed by the Rules Committee.

The Senate Committee on Rules and Administration also considers possible changes in the standing rules of the Senate, but it has no role in determining the order of business on the Senate floor.

★ ★ ★

Sergeant at Arms. The officer charged with maintaining order in the Chamber, under the direction of the presiding officer.

Session. Each Congress is composed of two sessions. A new session of Congress begins each January 3 at noon and continues until adjourned "sine die." (see *Adjournment Sine Die*)

Speaker. The presiding officer of the House of Representatives, elected by its members.

Special Session. A session of Congress, convened by the President of the United States or the leadership of both parties, after Congress has adjourned *sine die*. (see *Lame Duck Session*)

Strike Out the Last Word. A motion entitling Members of the House to speak for five minutes on a measure then being debated in the Chamber. A Member gains recognition by moving to strike out the last word of the amendment or section of the bill then under consideration—only a formality to address the House.

Sponsor. The Member who introduces a bill, amendment, motion, and the like.

Substitute. An amendment, or sometimes the text of an entire bill, introduced in place of the pending text. Passage of a substitute measure eliminates the original language by replacing it. Under certain circumstances, a substitute may be amended before being adopted.

Supplemental Appropriation. An appropriation to cover the difference between an agency's regular appropriation and the amount that becomes necessary for it to operate for the full fiscal year, because of new laws or obligations.

Suspension of the Rules. A time-saving House procedure for passing bills, usually reserved for noncontroversial measures. The motion, if agreed to by two-thirds of those present in the Chamber, suspends all rules which would otherwise prevent consideration of the pending matter. Debate is limited to 40 minutes and no amendments from the floor may be offered. If a two-thirds favorable vote is not attained, the bill may be considered later under regular procedures. This parliamentary procedure is in order only on Mondays and Tuesdays.

★ ★ ★

Table a Bill. An adverse procedure used by both bodies to lay to rest a matter they don't want to consider. A motion to "lay on the table" is not debatable in either House. Motions to table may be reconsidered.

★ ★ ★

Unanimous Consent Agreement. A procedure used frequently in both Houses to advance a proposition without resorting to the established rules of procedure. A single objection thwarts the unanimous consent agreement.

★ ★ ★

Veto. The refusal by the President to approve a bill or joint resolution submitted to him by Congress, other than one proposing an amendment to the Constitution. When Congress is in session, the President has 10 days in which to sign a bill, excluding Sundays; if he does not sign it, the bill automatically becomes law. When the President vetoes a bill, he returns it to the House of origin with a message stating his objections. In this case, it may be voted on again by Congress and, if approved by a two-thirds vote in both Houses, it becomes law despite the President's veto. (see *Override a Veto*)

★ ★ ★

Without Objection. (see *Unanimous Consent Agreement*)